D0287320

With Ears to Hear

With Ears to Hear

Preaching as Self-Persuasion

Robin R. Meyers

The Pilgrim Press
Cleveland, Ohio

The Pilgrim Press, Cleveland, Ohio 44115
© 1993 by Robin R. Meyers

Printed in the United States of America
The paper used in this publication is acid free and meets the
minimum requirements of American National Standard for
Information Sciences-Permanence of Paper for Printed Library
Materials, ANSI Z39.48—1984

98 97 96 95 94 93   5 4 3 2 1

Library of Congress Cataloging-in-Publication Data

Meyers, Robins R. (Robin Rex), 1952-
    With ears to hear : preaching as self-persuasion / Robin R.
  Meyers.
        p.   cm.
    Includes bibliographical references.
    ISBN 0-8298-0951-1
    1. Preaching. I. Title.
  BV4211.2.M42   1993
  251—dc20   92-42040
                                          CIP

In studying a sermon he [the preacher] ought to place himself in the situation of a serious hearer. Let him suppose the subject addressed to himself; let him consider what views of it would strike him most; what arguments would be most likely to persuade him; what parts of it would dwell most upon his mind. Let these be employed as his principal materials; and in these, it is most likely his genius will exert itself with the greatest vigour.

Hugh Blair
"Eloquence in the Pulpit"
Lectures on Rhetoric and Belles Lettres

Contents

Introduction

A SIMPLE IDEA FROM THE REAL WORLD

Whenever ministers gather to talk shop, sooner or later the conversation turns to preaching. Proclamation is at the center of the church's life, and every renewal of the church has been accompanied by a renewal in preaching. Few can survive the parish ministry without a strong sense of what it means to climb the stairs of the pulpit and tell people the secrets of their own hearts. Equally few can honestly say that preaching, however exciting on occasion, is not the most painful, tedious, and unpredictable thing they do on a regular basis.

Yet almost without exception, when clerics are asked to tell the story of their calling, they talk of a preacher whose sermons moved them deeply at a critical time in their lives. Many were sent packing off to seminary nursing a dream of becoming the heir apparent to some pulpit giant. But the road to that homiletic stardom was bumpy to say the least. Imitation won't do, because although it may be the sincerest form of flattery, it is dishonest and makes for a hollow sound in the soul. Mastering the mechanics of engaging speech won't do the trick—there are plenty of polished ad writers in the pulpit. And being theologically "sound" doesn't guarantee persuasiveness either. In fact, it often tempts one to be condescending and compromises the vital qualities of awe and wonder. What is it, then, that makes a preacher great? Can preaching be taught at all?

Most of us in homiletics are secretly terrified that Joseph Sittler has already answered that question, and the answer casts a long and discouraging shadow over all our work. But we also know intuitively that the stakes are too high for resignation. No one argues that preaching is not an art, as complex and mysterious as any art form can be. But we know that art, however elevated above the sum total of skill and technique, is nevertheless a product of the mother and father of all creativity: discipline.

Behind every great performance, out of sight like the ropes and pulleys of the stage, the scaffolding of persuasion is hours of practice, secret labor, and soul-searching critical reflection upon matters of form and content. Great preaching is neither a cosmic fluke nor a standard rhetorical equation where one size fits all. It is an *incarnation*, an event in the world of sound, words becoming flesh. As such, it is a phenomenon subject to analysis, and yet beyond analysis.

One thing is certain. When it happens, both the preacher and the congregation are blessed beyond measure—and likewise cursed by the dissatisfaction that a sampling of the sublime can create. Great expectations are both a blessing and a curse. The more preaching moves toward accomplishing what all sermons aim for, an experience of the ineffable, the more they create an appetite that is insatiable. The more gifted the preacher becomes, the more compulsive. The richer the food for those in the pews, the less likely they are to accept homiletic fast food. Whether we like it or not, we are undone by our own possibilities.

In the last thirty years, the field of homiletics has undergone a revolution. Old assumptions about what makes people hear the Word of God, which speech forms are most effective in the oral mode, and what rhetorical strategies engage the listener to assimilate and internalize faith have undergone dramatic change. Sermons that for centuries had been impaled on the deductive spikes of Greek rhetorical form were cut loose by a rediscovery of the inductive movement of narrative and poetry.

Oddly enough, modern homileticians did not discover something new. They went back to the text, which has been the first move in every renewal of the church, and found a neglected theory of human communication. The mystery of one's relationship to God cannot be captured in propositional form and passed directly from one human being to another—not even if the sermon is impeccably logical and flawlessly delivered. It must be wrapped, like faith itself, in the paradoxical distance and intimacy that stories provide, in the grandeur of myth, the lilt of songs, the memory of legend, and the seductive disorientation of parables. Preachers fail to communicate not because of *what* they say, but because of *how* they say it.

It became apparent to a new generation of preachers that an understanding of human communication theory is a primary concern, and that taking one's rhetorical clues from Scripture is an enlightened activity. In fact, it is the very essence of biblical preaching. The shape of the sermon ought not to be a living contradiction of the shape of the text from which it is drawn. Scripture is preserved as a canonized remnant of *encounter*. To turn it into an embellished argument, or an extended treatise on matters of doctrine or the inherent practicality of the life of faith, is a theological as well as a methodological aberration.

Ernest Campbell reminds us that sermons have to be more than truthful. They have to be interesting. They have to be more than "sound." They have to be beguiling. Above all, they have to be more than reasonable and prudent. Their function, like the text from which they germinate, is to disorient in order to reorient. The reason we preach is not simply to produce agreement or disagreement, as if to poll the heart or shore up the party. It is to shine the light of the Gospel upon the human situation and leave the listener amazed, frightened, inspired, undone.

These sweeping changes in homiletic theory were liberating to some and threatening to others. Poets felt vindicated while the inarticulate and unpoetic felt put upon. Great strides have been made in the last three decades toward eliminating the deadly fiction that form and content can be separated in human communication, or that somehow the sheer weight of the Gospel guarantees its own hearing. But the bad news is that no shortcuts exist, no sermon can be marked "Good for Any Occasion," and no preacher can fail to read or pretend to write. The new sermon forms make even greater demands upon the disciplines of creativity than did the old, standard outline forms. Some preachers have no doubt secretly longed for the days when all that sleepy listeners expected of the sermon was three points and a joke.

Yet having said this, there is still something missing from

homiletic theory these days. After the euphoria of narrative preaching faded and found itself in some quarters under outright attack, the teachers of preaching in this country settled into an uneasy peace. Traditionalists, whose training in rhetoric taught them to respect the discipline of a carefully crafted sermon, quietly suspected that "story preaching" had been oversold. After all, the notion that narrative is for incidental embellishment and cannot carry the heavy freight of the Gospel dies hard. Mothers who suspect their children of lying still say, "Are you *storying* to me?"

On the other hand, those who gladly called themselves "story preachers" often failed to understand that when narrative preaching offers itself up as an excuse for lack of preparation or degenerates into sloppy, sentimental, and overly autobiographical excursions into slice-of-life or stream-of-consciousness rambling, it can be even worse than dry expositions on matters of doctrine. After all, the listeners could at least assume that the latter was about something important.

Perhaps this disagreement over form may be pushing homiletics in a new direction, suggesting that a far more elusive quality may be responsible for great preaching. This quality is hard to describe without misunderstanding because the only word available is, like so many venerable words, obscured by a multitude of meanings. It is word that describes the momentary insanity of criminals as well as the delirium of lovers. It is said to make us interesting on the one hand, dangerous on the other. Without it, life becomes an endless afternoon, a flat, tedious stretch of mindless motion. The word is *passion*.

One can hardly imagine a professor of homiletics who would argue with this statement: there is no persuasion without passion. Passion makes us persuasive. Be it the first sermon on wobbly knees, or the final sermon of some preacher emeritus, everyone wants to get and keep what cannot be prescribed or purchased. It is that energy for communicating the Gospel that keeps the call to ministry from becoming a mere profession, and that mysterious compulsion to preach the Word from degenerating into the obligatory duties of an ecclesiastical master of ceremonies.

The obvious question then becomes: if sermonic passion is so universally vital to good preaching, why has no one ever attempted to uncover a *mode* of communication that creates and sustains it? Perhaps the debates over form and content, important as they are, would seem pale by comparison to discovering a means by which sermonic passion is generated and sustained. In fact, such a discovery might go a long way toward instructing preachers about form and content—if only someone could suggest a method of preaching that generated passion.

Yet who dares to be so bold? Isn't passion one of those qualities that like faith is as unapproachable as it is inexplicable? Do we not regard it as so far removed from the world of advice and consent as to render it beyond human engineering—either a curse or a matter of grace? And does this not leave us in a quandary, a situation in which something vital to our art is considered for all practical purposes unattainable by human design? In other words, is passion something we must have but can't acquire?

I would gladly resign myself to the ranks of those who pass when it comes to such conjecture, except for one disquieting fact: I must preach every week in a local church. That means that sermonic passion is no peripheral, academic concern. It is not my wish to climb into the pulpit every Sunday and report the Gospel. My wish is to create an appetite for the Gospel and to make the satisfying of that appetite contagious. Without authentic passion on my part, preaching becomes either the ultimate arrogance or the ultimate futility. Arrogant by virtue of presuming to know the value of something I have never tried; futile by virtue of trying to sound like I care when I don't.

So here is the motivation for writing these words: I believe that a mode of preaching really exists by which authentic passion can be created and sustained. It is, in fact, as much a state of mind *about* preaching as it is a particular methodology. It involves a fundamental shift in the preacher's perception of the nature and purpose of the sermon. And like most meaningful insights, this revelation came in a rather ordinary but unexpected way.

Two apparently unrelated ideas converged to compel the writing of these words. The first is a comment that can be heard at just about any preaching conference or gathering of clergy in the country. When ministers talk of the love/hate relationship they have with the pulpit and reflect on one of those moments when something unexpectedly rich or effective took place, perhaps to their surprise, they will often say something like this: *"It was almost like I was preaching to myself."*

The second idea came in the context of formal education: a persuasion theory class at the University of Oklahoma. On one slow and tedious afternoon, just when I was about to lose all contact between the language of persuasion research and the mysterious process known as attitude change, a quotation cut through the air and took my sleepy mind by storm. It was, like all the best ideas, both utterly simple and richly germinal. Herbert Simmons, describing what he considers to be the dominant role played by the recipient of a persuasion message, said this: "In a real sense, we do not persuade others at all; we only provide the stimulus with which they persuade themselves."[1]

If this is true, and if ministers are unconsciously insightful when they speak of good sermons as acts of self-persuasion, then perhaps it is because homiletic intuition and experimental social psychology have unwittingly merged common sense with laboratory results in the name of a new and compelling metaphor for human communication.

If it is true that when the stakes are high (and in preaching they always are) we must persuade *ourselves* of the most important things, then preachers cannot, and should not, be exempt from the experience of their own sermons. If every sermon were viewed as an intentional act of self-persuasion, our Holy Grail of sermonic passion might well be the result of the preacher's own authentic struggle with the text. In fact, if self-persuasion is the name of the game for everyone who encounters the radical demands of the Gospel, then what the people in the pews need is a *model self-persuader*. In other words, the best way to persuade the people is to persuade the toughest customer the Gospel has: the preacher.

Chapter 1
What Is Self-Persuasion?

Of what use is a gold key if it will not open what we wish? Or what objection is there to a wooden one which will, when we seek nothing except to open what is closed? But since there is some comparison between eating and learning, it may be noted that on account of the fastidiousness of many even that food without which life is impossible must be seasoned.

—Saint Augustine

The Rocky Marriage of Rhetoric and Homiletics

As early as the fourth century, Saint Augustine was adapting the rhetoric of Cicero to the problems of the pulpit, trying to persuade preachers that the truth of the Gospel was not self-evident. As bishop of Hippo, Augustine found himself perplexed by one of the church's perennial dilemmas: preachers who assume that because they traffic in truth, they need not use maps. Instead, they believed, matters of ultimate concern would somehow communicate themselves. Besides, the church is "in the world, but not of it," and those amoral sophists had proved that a silver tongue is no guarantee of righteousness.

A reformed hedonist of the first magnitude who used to pray for delays in any conversion that might crimp his style, Augustine knew all too well the corruptible nature of persuasion. Quoting Cicero, he reminded his preachers, "Wisdom without eloquence is of small benefit to states; but eloquence without wisdom is often extremely injurious and profits no one."[1] Just the same, such noble sentiments did nothing to improve the preaching of his time. Then, as now, it was often atrociously boring.

This dilemma, appearing on the surface to be little more than a bishop's muse over that elusive thing we call great preaching, is really indicative of a deeper, centuries-old ambivalence between rhetoric and homiletics—the oldest marriage in the field of human communication. Can the persuasive arts be learned and practiced in service to a higher truth, or do they inevitably tempt the user to substitute style for substance? Augustine made it clear that if one had to choose between wisdom and eloquence, he preferred clumsy truth to articulate evil. But in resigning himself to this dichotomy, he fell victim to one of the oldest and most venerable schisms in communication theory: the artificial separation of form and content.

The fiction remains strong among us even today that *what* one says can be easily separated from *how* one says it. Further, that the brightest minds have always traded in matter, not manner. When was the last time a scholar from the ivory-tower world of What walked across the street to audit a class in the vo-tech world of How? The heavy brows ask the heavy questions: What are the facts? What is the truth? What do we believe? Once the pipe smoke has cleared the room, no sensible person dares to ask, "But how? . . . *How* is the truth communicated, appropriated, and practiced?" The question will be met with stony silence, if not sneers of derision. Let this curious student teach "Applied Science," or, in the seminary, "Practical Theology" (as if there is any other kind).

Perhaps this is exaggerated, but the problem is real. For preachers, any dismissal of form as inferior to content is deadly for the pulpit. Classical rhetoric, after all, had emphasized form. Only two of the classical canons refer to content (inventio and dispositio), while the other three had to do with delivery (elocutio, memoria, and actio). Why then do we continue to believe that "getting up" a sermon is more important than getting one out? Fred Craddock writes:

> "How" is for many an ugly word, a cause of embarrassment. There is large opinion that "how" is to be found not among prophets or philosophers, but among mechanics and carpenters. After all, does not "how" introduce methods and skills more appropriate to a course in driver training than to probing

into the mysteries of ultimate reatilty? What has skill got to do
with the kingdom of God?[2]

Some ministers are even guilty of believing that ultimate truth
communicates itself by virtue of its being ultimate, when in fact
the opposite may be true. The more important, the more intimate, the more profound the subject matter, the harder it is for
one person to communicate it directly to another. Søren
Kierkegaard is right: "Truth is not nimble on its feet . . . it is not
its own evangelist."

What is the answer then? A return to persuasion as science?
Should preachers who know *what* but do not know *how* enroll
again in Aristotle 101, memorizing the *topoi*, arming themselves
with elaborate persuasive strategies that promise to produce the
desired results if all the right rhetorical buttons are pushed? The
problem with this approach is that in preaching, one rhetorical
size does *not* fit all.

When Aristotle wrote his classic definition of rhetoric ("The
faculty of discovering in every case the available means of persuasion"[3]), he used language that is essentially presumptive. Words
like *in every case* and *means* infer that in every persuasive situation, a strategy exists and need merely be found. Like a rhetorical
match made in heaven, for every problem of speaker, context,
and purpose, some answer exists, wrapped in the perfect combi-
nation of syllogistic logic, deductive movement, and appropriate
delivery. It was all so scientific.

But persuasion is more art than science, and there is abundant
evidence to suggest that people don't necessarily believe things
just because they are true—not even when they are logical, well
illustrated, and beautifully spoken. Preachers are concerned not
with assent but with appropriation. A thumbs-up or thumbs-
down in the assembly at Athens is one thing, but a "heart
strangely warmed" is a little harder to measure. Guilt or inno-
cence can be voted on, but how does one register charity?

The nature of the Gospel is not propositional. The Bible is not
some sort of giant index of doctrinal syllogisms, cross-referenced
for the proof-texting preacher. It is a tapestry of encounters between human beings and God, woven over thousands of years

with the threads of myth, ancient cosmology, and particular culture. It is a Story, preserved for the sake of religious self-understanding, gathered and canonized to prevent spiritual amnesia and to guard against false teaching.

When Paul took this Story into the Hellenistic world, the very nature of preaching shifted—from narratives designed to pull the listener into an experience of the truth, to embellished arguments designed to get people to accept or reject Christianity. For centuries this shift helped define the sermon by virtue of a classic form: "Since the time of Origen a sermon has been an extended argument with a sophistic style employing rhetorical questions, exclamations, contrasts, and exaggerations, all clothed in a prolixity of images and metaphors."[4]

Yet once a story has become an argument, more than literary form has changed—so has the very nature of the listener's responsibility. Narrative speech forms create an entirely different experience in the listener than does propositional discourse. The former demands participation and resolution, whereas the latter appeals primarily to the detached process of intellectual assent.

It is not difficult to understand why rhetoric and homiletics joined early for noble purposes and then quarrelled bitterly for centuries. Our purpose here is not to counsel separation, and certainly not to call for divorce. Any preacher who does not study rhetoric assumes that the historic insights into the cause and effect of the human utterance are without redeeming value. On the other hand, the rules of engaging and logical speech alone cannot communicate the mystery of the Incarnation. For one thing, unconditional love isn't logical, nor does faith come at the end of a major and minor premise.

However appealing it may seem, preachers are not, as were the classical rhetors of old, master archers—shaping the arrows of the persuasive message, embellishing it with brightly colored enthymemes, dipping it in just the right brand of logical curative, and standing tall to aim and fire with conviction. In fact, God seems to have ordained that persuasion is much more complicated than this, and that nothing about the Gospel is guaranteed to "work on contact."

The Rise of Listener-Centered Theory

It should come as no surprise to those who read and write in the field of preaching that the break from Aristotle's message-centered view of persuasion came from the pen of three clergymen. Hugh Blair was minister of the High Church in Edinburgh, George Campbell was a Scottish Presbyterian cleric, and Richard Whately was archbishop of Dublin. All three made significant contributions during the so-called British period in rhetoric, more aptly named the "psychological" by Douglas Ehninger.[5] These preachers responded to the pressure of the Enlightenment upon Christian hermeneutics by shifting their concern in persuasion from the mouth to the ear.

The writing of Bacon, Descartes, Locke, Hume, and other epistemologists, along with the rise of faculty psychology, caused rhetors to shift their emphasis away from what a message does to a listener and toward what a listener does with a message. The Age of Reason had eroded traditional religious authority and undermined orthodox assumptions about preaching. Gone were the days when something was considered true because it was spoken from a pulpit. It became increasingly necessary to make Christianity sound reasonable and enlightened, not just ancient and mystical.

Blair wrote that the supreme goal in communication (to motivate the will) required a careful distinction between persuasion and mere conviction. Campbell added to Locke's categories of understanding and will those of imagination and passion. To effect genuine attitude change, and to motivate action based on a new set of values, Christian rhetoric had to do more than instruct, please, or even edify. It had to act as a catalyst. Reason alone, though nearly deified in the seventeenth and eighteenth centuries, could not accomplish what Campbell considered the final act of persuasion:

> It is not therefore the understanding alone that is here concerned. If the orator would prove successful, it is necessary that he engage in his service all these different powers of the mind, the imagination, the memory, and the passions. These are not the supplanters of reason, or even rivals in her sway: they are

her handmaids, by whose ministry she is enabled to usher truth
into the heart, and procure it there a favorable reception.[6]

In trying to reconcile passion and logic in preaching, Campbell and others paved the way for what have come to be called
active participation theories of persuasion. Instead of regarding
the listener as a passive victim of the message (the so-called
hypodermic-needle approach), the more contemporary theories
regard the listener as an active, even obstinate partner, selecting
and interacting with messages on his or her own terms.

As long as the listener is acting in an atmosphere of perceived
choice (which distinguishes persuasion from coercion), the process is really best described as *self-persuasion*. Experimental social
psychologists coined this simple term to designate an alternative
notion to that of human beings as information processors. That
is, instead of being manipulated by a message, research has
shown that people take an active, even dominant role in manipulating the message. A modern persuasion theorist, who uses the
term *self-persuasion* to describe the process at work in all active
participation models, talks about "the internalization or volun-
tary acceptance of new cognitive states or patterns of overt behavior through the exchange of messages."[7]

Notice the final phrase, "through the *exchange* of messages."
The assumption here is that the listener responds by creating
messages of his or her own and then assigning meaning to those
messages. Anthony Greenwald and his associates have done
studies that suggest that people typically engage in active, covert
argumentation in response to externally generated messages.
These messages are often idiosyncratic and take the form of both
supportive and counter argumentation.[8] If this sounds very much
like talking to oneself, it is exactly that.

Self-persuasion is simply a term used to describe a complex set
of responses that locate persuasive effect in listener-generated
messages. Far from a state of passively receiving and being manipulated by external messages, self-persuasion describes what
happens when a message gets people talking to themselves. It
suggests that persuasion is finally a self-generated, rather than an
other-generated phenomenon.

Although it is typical to think of persuasion as a speaker's effort to change a listener's attitude, self-persuasion suggests that speakers can get people to talk themselves into or out of attitudes by using the original message as a stimulus. The object is to elicit a kind of authoritative *intra*personal conversation in the listener. The question may no longer be "Are you listening to me?" but "Does listening to me get you talking to yourself?"

Abraham Tesser conducted studies once that proved that "mere thought" can change attitudes. That is, just by asking people to think about some issue, without any outside inducement, a significant strengthening of the initial attitudes about the issue took place. The longer people thought, the greater the number of covert arguments they generated, and the more marked were the self-persuasive effects.[9]

The significance of these studies is obvious. If it is possible for people to change their attitudes merely by thinking about some issue, then traditional, message-centered theories of persuasion left out something very important. Among both social psychologists and communication theorists, the notion that persuasion is transactional in nature, process-oriented, and response dependent is now firmly rooted in research. If taken seriously by those who preach, and by those who are preached at, self-persuasion changes the very nature of the game.

What Difference Does It Make?

Most homiletic wisdom has been infused with the notion that the preacher persuades, that the good sermon persuades, and that most of all, the good preacher preaching the good sermon persuades. It is a product mentality, reinforced by a consumer mentality. Deliver the goods, and the people will buy. But what if the self-persuasion theorists are right? What if we aren't delivering rhetorical goods, but rather creating rhetorical experiences in which the listeners are the real producers? The first models of communication were drawn by telephone company engineers. Not surprisingly, they were linear, with a source, a medium, and a receiver. What interfered with the message, of course, was called *noise*. It was all one-way, until someone came up with the concept of *feedback*. This was supposed to be something coming back from the listener, helping the speaker discern how well the message had worked. No one thought that feedback might be something listeners got from themselves, or speakers received by overhearing their own speech!

This whole idea is a bit unsettling, if not heretical. It sounds as if we are talking about relinquishing all responsibility for the communication process, reducing the great and noble art of sermonizing to a tenuous, mumbling shot in the rhetorical darkness. How is one to know for sure that listeners have started talking to themselves? Who is to say that the preacher caused it? And what about all those sacred notions of authority, of the objective quality of the Word of God, and of the orthodox view of the listener as accepting or rejecting the truth rather than having the audacity to rephrase it?

These are formidable questions, and one is tempted to scurry back to the relative comfort of a message-centered approach. After all, one can be the architect of a beautiful sermon and simply ask that its form and content be judged. But who wants to start second-guessing what sort of private conversations people are having as a result of what they hear? And besides, doesn't this all but negate the importance of the original, external message?

Self-persuasion theorists would never argue that a good sermon is about getting people to talk to themselves about just anything. They would argue that it is about getting them to talk to themselves in specific ways about specific things. The preacher still sets the agenda, chooses the subject matter, and directs the conversation by virtue of what he chooses to say, or not say. The sermon sets the table and invites the listener to dine. But the preacher has no intention of serving food to be consumed in awkward, obligatory silence. He has provided a feast for the purpose of conversation. Some of the guests have no doubt brought food of their own. Others are comfortable enough to comment upon what is put before them. But no dinner party is a monologue, and no worthwhile sermon ought to be one either.

The problem is that most sermons *are* monologues. The preacher is the only one talking. How, then, is it possible to construct a sermon that possesses the essential quality of dialogue and by its very nature compels the listeners to respond with messages of their own?

The answer may lie in the process of self-persuasion itself. That is, if listeners are expected to self-persuade, why should the preacher be exempt from the same process? If it is self-persuasion the preacher wants, why shouldn't it be self-persuasion that the preacher models? In other words, what if preachers viewed their sermons as *intentional acts of self-persuasion?*

Again, the mind has a tendency to seize upon a cartoon: the preacher talking to herself in front of a lot of bewildered, embarrassed people. But self-persuasion from the preacher's point of view would not consist of public acts of intrapersonal dialogue— that would be unbearable. What it would mean is that the preacher would engage the text as fully for her own sake as for that of her congregation. She would produce sermons that she also intended to consume, engaging her ear as fully as her mouth. She would breathe in the very words she breathed out, responding to what she hears herself say with amazement, confusion, sorrow, delight, anger, fear, and wonder.

Simple and strange as it may sound, what is suggested here is that preachers *participate* in their own sermons, not just deliver them. Their dialect would become a model for the dialectic of the listener. Their conversations with the text, with the world, and with themselves would become a model of what sermonic language can do to someone who is emotionally and intellectually alive. Lest we forget, the delight in listening to a great teller of jokes lies in watching the joy of the teller. Every great weaver of tales listens to himself with the same pleasure he means to evoke from his listener.

This idea is too intriguing not to expand. It spirals outward and gathers in some of the most fundamental issues in preaching. It is a mind-set as much as a methodology, an attitude as much as a paradigm. It might just rescue the sermon event for a very important person in the sanctuary—the preacher. And in the process, it could help to recover authenticity and relevance as a measure of personal honesty. After all, the first person to be bored and the first person to be inspired would be the same person who had created either condition.

The rest of these pages will be concerned with the implications of an affirmative answer to this question: *Can preaching be regarded with benefit as an intentional act of self-persuasion?* We will consider first a number of operating assumptions that make it possible to even ask the question. What would one have to assume about the nature of faith, for example, in order to regard preaching as an act of self-persuasion? What about the role of the listener, the interpretation of Scripture, the nature of authority, and the person of the preacher? Finally, such an approach will be translated from the theoretical to the practical, offering concrete advice on the use of language, dialectic, and a hitherto unexplored homiletic concept: vicariousness.

Chapter 2
Self-Persuasion and the Nature of Faith

To this end come those who have lost the passion for their task and who now no longer preach and teach the gospel but who drop the names of famous persons endorsing the product, extol the contributions of Christianity to our civilization, urge attendance to duties, and occasionally scold the absentees.

—Fred B. Craddock

Kierkegaard's Elusive Christianity

Danish philosopher Søren Kierkegaard spent the whole of his eccentric life pushing on the edges of the absurd, writing bizarre parables and whimsical essays that examined the follies of social convention, the irrationalities of decency, and most of all, the comic pity of an easy faith. The greatest gulf in human life, he wrote, is that between *concept* and *capacity*. We can read a good book on grace, but that does not make us gracious. The longest trip a person ever takes is the journey between head and heart.

Kierkegaard found it absurd that the church had taken the Gospel and turned it into a piece of information, assuming that character followed cognition without an existential experience. The Story had been distilled into a list of essential doctrines, and faith was defined by signing on, not by venturing out. The biblical characters of flesh and blood, who tasted life on both sides of the covenant and scratched out on parchment their misery and their ecstasy, became plaster saints on the ceilings of great cathedrals where drowsy worshippers took the leap of faith with a quiet nod.

People are not saved, said Kierkegaard, by the things they know but by the ideas they live. This, after all, is the lesson of the Incarnation. Much of what Jesus taught was not new, but the way in which the "word became flesh" made it seem that way. Faith in Denmark in those days was an easy and fashionable thing, requiring only intellectual assent and membership by birth certificate. Yet without struggle, introspection, and self-denial, there is no faith. Likewise with honest doubt: to have the capacity for it is to require the faith that overcomes it.

Besides, the availability of truth is no guarantee of its appropriation, as any teacher knows who walks the lonely aisles of the library. The student must have an appetite for knowledge, a need for it that goes beyond the coercion of the assignment. On this point, preachers are particularly susceptible to a kind of homiletic fatigue. They quickly forget whether they are preaching because they want to or because they have to.

How quickly the calling turns into a profession, the eagerness to preach into an obligation to preach. Paid to dispense Christian Information, the pulpit becomes one more chore and its occupant a hireling. Stuck with the thankless job of filling the sanctuary with words no one will hear, much less believe, the preacher begins to rationalize his failures by blaming both lack of time and the dull ears of those who "won't listen." The real problem may be that the preacher has quit listening.

Kierkegaard understood that ministers are particularly susceptible to the illusion that the Gospel is a commodity. In other words, what they presume to own they sell by increments to a captive customer. It is assumed that as preachers they have paid off their spiritual note (after all, are they not ordained?), and that what the kingdom needs is more liens against it. The effect can be insidious for preacher and listener alike. Each believes that to extol the product is the same thing as using it. One of Kierkegaard's most famous parables laments the fact that there is something about constantly *recommending* the good that seems to diminish the speaker's obligation to *be* good. He compares this condition to a man who smiles and waves to everyone he sees, as if to greet and engage them, while all the time walking backwards—facing them, but moving away.[1]

If faith is the sort of thing one pursues but never fully acquires, then the notion of preaching as self-persuasion may be truly useful. If the listener is to be constantly in training, then why not the minister as well? If this seems to undermine the notion of authority, consider which is more subversive to faith: honest struggle or premature righteousness? And since the gap between preachers and those in the pews is already exaggerated by stereotypes, elevated pulpits, and the unanswered power of monologue, shouldn't we move in the direction that overcomes distance rather than adds to it?

All of this raises ancient debates within the church about the relationship between the Gospel and the faith of the preacher. Nobody wants to make the case that the tale is completely dependent on the teller, but honesty demands that we admit the inseparability of message and messenger—at least as far as effective communication is concerned. So the question becomes: how close to the Gospel do we stand, at the risk of being trivial and self-indulgent; or how far away do we stand, at the risk of losing authenticity and passion?

Nobody wants a talking head in the pulpit, a detached and mechanical dispenser of cue-card morality. But neither does anyone really want to believe that the Gospel rises and falls solely on personality, lifestyle, or even momentary moods. Just the same, preaching is an enormously intimate act, and preachers are what Kiekegaard calls "town criers of inwardness." Too much detachment is deadly and will cause resentment in the listener. Human beings can sense immediately if a speaker has exempted himself from the struggles he is recommending for others. This is precisely why preaching as self-persuasion offers a new approach to the problems of faith, intimacy, and distance.

What could be worse than a preacher who appears to have finished the race and is now exhorting the rest of us from the sideline? Or perhaps a better analogy is the captain of a sculling team—once in a while she should turn around, take up the oars, and face the spot where she once barked her commands. When it comes to the Gospel, we are all walking around a mountain too high to climb. What we need is a rhetorical trail guide, a word-scout, someone willing to go on ahead and come back with a report, not someone who simply condenses and distributes the view from the top.

To consider every sermon an act of self-persuasion is not to diminish either the independent authority of the Gospel or the vital role of the preacher's faith. The preacher self-persuades because the Gospel is true, whether he manages to live it or not. But by not exempting himself from the struggle, he gives hope and encouragement to all who struggle with him. This process is both intrinsically personal and appropriately humble. Personal because the preacher is intentional about experiencing what the listener experiences and humble because a struggle by nature compliments the desirability of the goal without presuming to have reached it.

As for passion, that most important ingredient of all—how could any preacher be expected to maintain energy for that which has already been accomplished? Although many in the church today view salvation as a sudden, permanent, born-again experience, Kierkegaard spoke wisely when he said that a man had to convince himself of the truth of the Gospel every single morning. One can only assume that he did not intend to exclude the preacher.

The Renewing Quality of Rhetoric

One might object to the idea of self-persuasion on the grounds that preachers ought to know what they believe before they start speaking, so what is the point of listening to one's own sermon? Isn't that a little like reading one's own book? Not exactly, according to much recent work in the philosophy of language. The very "act" of verbalizing a thought or idea has a certain intensifying and reinforcing effect upon the speaker. When the subject matter is faith, the need to hear oneself say what it is that one believes becomes even more acute. R. E. C. Browne writes:

> To preach is a profound necessity for the preacher's own development. A preacher's interior life must be expressed in appropriate overt acts or it degenerates into a delicate private soul-culture. Preaching is one of the most significant activities by which a preacher gives freely what he has been freely given.[2]

In recent years, biblical scholars as well as homileticians have reminded us that preaching is an oral/aural phenomenon. Traditional homiletics has focused upon the sermon as the exposition of a text, conditioned first by the eye and not by the ear. Yet, as Walter Ong has testified, it is absurd to try to understand the effect of the spoken word by applying the paradigms of print. He compares it to "thinking of horses as automobiles with wheels."[3]

Perhaps the single biggest failure in the teaching of preaching is that young ministers are not fully impressed with the difference between textuality and orality. Shaped by mountains of books, called upon to write scores of papers, and graded largely by what they commit to the page, aspiring preachers train the eye but neglect the ear. Yet it is into the world of sound that they will go, plying their wares acoustically. The major moments of public ministry (the sermon, the funeral eulogy, the marriage ceremony) are all rhetorical moments. No one will see their outlines, much less grade them. Rather, as Jesus warned, "By their *words* they will be justified, by their *words* they will be condemned."

The spoken word is not static, nor can it be recovered, except in memory. It occurs in a moment of time and resonates between living persons. It implies what it builds—relationships in community. Further, words are not just a bag of tools for reporting on the world. They *do* something; they are acts. Thanks to the work of Austin and Searle, among others, we know that the spoken word has "performative" power. Life itself offers up abundant examples: marriage vows commit, the sentence of a judge incarcerates, the declaration of knighthood transforms the ordinary warrior—all by the delicate and tenuous vibration of air over eardrums.

For the preacher, not only must the difference between eye and ear be understood, but the capacity of rhetoric to renew as well. Heidegger has called language "the house of being," and he quotes Holderlin to make a crucial point: "Therefore has language, most dangerous of possessions, been given to man . . . so that he may *affirm* what he is."[4] Not only does the spoken word commit us, but it reminds us as well. Especially when the subject matter is of ultimate concern, to hear one's own words is to be reminded of what one believes, again and again. In one important sense, preaching the Gospel is an imaginative act of repetition.

Much has been written about the "dead air of familiarity" that surrounds a two-thousand-year-old pulpit.[5] But preaching as self-persuasion might be able to turn the liability of repetition into an asset. After all, repetition is only dangerous when words become incantation, flowing from programmed worshippers in a deadly drone. Otherwise, to hear oneself say, out loud, what it is that one believes is powerful, even if we have heard it before.

People don't come to church to hear new things said in new ways, but to hear old things said in new ways. It's not that discovery is inappropriate, its just that congregations are sustained by what they already know. What they need to hear is new ways of knowing it, new lyrics that are grounded in dependable refrains. And most of all, they need to hear the preacher sing along.

In fact, the extent to which the preacher sings both the melody and the refrain will determine how ready and willing the congregation is to harmonize. The self-persuading sermon is almost like a soliloquy, where private thoughts given public utterance spark the same dialectic in the listener. But we are getting ahead of ourselves. For now, it is important to remember that the act of speaking one's faith can be an act of renewal, and that to talk out loud about important things in the presence of a community shaped by such utterances not only reminds and renews, it also commits. That is, to speak in certain ways is to be obligated in certain ways.

There is a reason why children repeat *ad nauseam* the oaths and secret sayings of membership in the imaginary societies of youth. Often, when a member's status is in question, the others will demand that readmission involve repetition of the oath, verbatim and without error. Athletes mumble encouragement to themselves at the starting line, saying over and over, "I can do it. . . . I can win. . . . I *am* the best." It isn't new information they're after but the sound of their own confidence vibrating against their own ear.

An increasingly popular tradition for the renewal of marriage is to speak again the original vows. Why not just agree to be committed in the privacy of one's heart? Because saying it matters. More than this, breaking the silence on behalf of what we believe marks out the strength of that belief. Contrary to much popular wisdom about the harmlessness of words (talk is cheap . . . talk is small), the fact is that speaking about important matters is painful and risky. Ask any father of a teenage son what frightens him most about their relationship, and he will probably talk about the silence that has descended between them. Counselors know that marriages are ended not only *in* silence, but *by* silence. And there is good reason why lovers are both desperate to hear, and yet paranoid about speaking three little words: "I love you."

Saying It, Hearing It, Believing It

Folk wisdom dictates that if something is really important, we should "put it in writing." But the spoken word binds us to each other by virtue of the fact that what proceeds out of one's mouth is tied inextricably to one's honor and integrity. There was a time when to give someone "your word" was to give them something infinitely more important than a signature on a contract. A child still exercises her greatest leverage over a parent by saying, simply, "But you *said!*" A politician lives to regret most the empty promises that could not be kept, because, after all, he is reminded again and again, "In the campaign you *said* . . ."

When Jesus asks Peter for a confession, he doesn't want it in writing. He demands that it come forth from out of Peter's mouth—not a report of what others have said but something much more difficult and profound: "Who do *you* say that I am?" It is interesting that the emphasis of that famous confession has always been more personal than rhetorical. That is, the existential dimension is always lifted up, because in matters of faith only the individual can decide. But the question also demands verbalization: "Who do you *say* that I am?" Say it for me to hear; say it for the world to hear; but most of all, say it for *yourself* to hear.

French existential phenomenologist Georges Gusdorf has said, "Whoever finds and speaks the right word is involved in creation out of chaos, and that whoever keeps his word creates value in the world."[6] Preachers must be concerned with both these aspects. First, because ordination compels the breaking of silence, and second, because every sermon commits the preacher to a certain level of fidelity. A sermon does more than instruct and inspire, it binds up. It does more than clarify and edify, it also subverts. With hearing comes accountability, as Jesus reminded us in those unsettling words from John: "If I had not come and spoken to them, they would not have sin; but now they have no excuse for their sin" (15:22).

When the writer of Matthew's Gospel describes the movement from revelation to proclamation as "What you hear whispered, proclaim from the housetops" (10:27), he is describing more than the nature of preaching. He is describing the compulsion of it as well. Faith by nature may originate in trembling silence, broken by revelations not obvious (or even audible) to everyone—the whisper. But it moves the faithful to a compulsive and reckless kind of behavior—the shout.[7] Although we have often talked about the compulsion to preach as it relates to the desire of the speaker to convert those listening, we have seldom spoken of it as an almost subconscious desire for the speaker to hear himself shout what God has only whispered.

Too often we accept the bromide that believing something means never having to talk about it. In our culture, the "strong silent type" is supposed to epitomize the holding of convictions with such strength and confidence that expression is unnecessary. But there is a difference between chatter and the compulsions of meaningful speech. Preaching as self-persuasion puts a whole new twist on Austin's "perlocutionary act"—speech designed to affect the feelings, attitudes, beliefs, or behaviors of listeners.[8] It assumes that the speaker is also a listener, and that one's own words can affect one's own feelings.

Even before the cowardly lion in *The Wizard of Oz* said to himself: "I do believe in spooks, I do believe in spooks, I do I do I do!" we have known that self-persuasion is part of the behavior of everyday life. In fact, the whole business of intrapersonal communication (talking to oneself) is fascinating. We have a need to rehearse our thoughts out loud, even if no one else is present to hear them. There is a reason why homeless people often mumble in steady steams of conversation meant for no one in particular: conversation is a necessity of life.

Plato's simple assertion that when the mind is thinking it is talking to itself speaks volumes about the intimate connection between thought and expression. Talking is very much like thinking out loud, and thinking is very much like talking to oneself. Alfred North Whitehead once pursued the notion that an organic connection exists between the brain and the vocal folds,[9] and philosophers debate whether reality even exists at all independent of our language-based system of meaning. Most scholars would agree that intention and meaning are the principal preoccupations of philosophy—hence the maddening problems of semantic circles and their infinite regressions.

Our concern here is not which came first, the word or the thought, or whether reality is "linguistically constituted" as Heidegger would say, but with the implications of the spoken word upon faith development. The quiet chemistry of thought, however amazing, is not to be compared with the turning loose of words, especially when the voice is near and dear, and the subject matter is profound.

Again, let the world of everyday experience be our teacher. What does the adolescent boy do before calling his girlfriend on the phone to ask for a date? If he is unsure of her response, he will carefully rehearse the conversation a dozen times. This way he can ask her out without asking her out, and in listening to himself, pick just the right persona. Should he be bold, casual, or shy and understated? Should he act as if her response really matters, or be cool enough to pretend that it doesn't? He checks the voice; he checks the phrasing. Don't be too cool, he thinks, or you will sound flippant. Don't be too serious, or you will sound desperate and vulnerable. By talking to himself, he gets a chance to hear how he sounds before he has to sound that way. Furthermore, he listens as if he were the girl and can therefore try on different personalities in the search for just the right rhetorical strategy.

As adults, we continue the process of rehearsing our thoughts and overhearing our attitudes. A communication researcher, Daryl Bem, has found that people infer their beliefs to some degree from their behaviors. They perform a sort of behavioral inventory, asking themselves what a certain behavior implies about their attitudes. [10] If the basic tenets of speech act theory are correct, sermons might be viewed as regular occasions for inferring beliefs based on rhetorical actions. Week after week, the preacher hears himself not only *saying* something about faith, but in so doing, engaging in an *act* of faith. Listening to himself, in a sense, he observes himself. So that's what I believe? And that's how I sound believing it?

Chapter 3
Self-Persuasion and the Listener

The most dramatic change in general communication theory during the last forty years has been the gradual abandonment of the idea of a passive audience, and its replacement by the concept of a highly active, highly selective audience, manipulating rather than being manipulated by a message.

—Wilber Schramm

At the Mouth or at the Ear?

For as long as scholars have studied the art and science of oral persuasion, they have put the principle burden for the success or failure of any persuasion attempt upon the speaker, the message, and the mechanics of delivery. They were "message-centered," as communication scholars would say. Since Aristotle, rhetoric has been preoccupied with the science of message construction. Audiences were analyzed, logical strategies selected, appropriate tropes and figures were hung on the speech like ornaments on a Christmas tree, and a mode of delivery was chosen to maximize the persuasive effect. For the most part, messages did something *to* listeners; listeners did not do something *with* messages.

In fact, it is difficult to read much traditional rhetorical theory without getting the impression that the listener was little more than a target. Like knock-down ducks at a carnival shooting gallery, some were young, some old, some educated, some ignorant, all sporting a different stripe by virtue of gender, group affiliation, and social class. They were moving targets to be sure, but they were regarded as largely passive victims of the right rhetorical aim. Even as late as the 1940s, when the famous Yale studies were conducted, communications scholars were still talking about people processing information as if they were machines rather than emotive, interactive human beings.[1]

In fact, these studies were largely motivated by Hitler's propaganda successes and funded by an American government determined not to be left behind in the race for the control of the public mind. The so-called hypodermic-needle approach to persuasion describes the view that people can be persuaded against their will, "injected" with a persuasive message much as a drug is administered with a syringe.

It was to counter such simplistic claims that so-called active-participation models of persuasion arose, mostly in the 1960s, 1970s, and 1980s. And the unifying, generic term that lumps them together is *self-persuasion*. Unfortunately, the whole concept suffers from the persistent misunderstanding that self-persuasion renders the message and the messenger benign, if not unnecessary. On the contrary, the importance of message construction remains, but it is driven by a belief that the listener is responsible for the ultimate persuasive effect. In the language of Kenneth Burke, the rhetor still sets the scene and directs the rhetorical drama. But the final act belongs to the listener, whose private, idiosyncratic conversations have been sparked by a conversational preacher. In self-persuasion, the last thing a preacher wants to have is the last word.

The sermon becomes a trip, not a destination. It goes beyond ornamental briefs on the human condition and becomes, instead, a walking tour full of bright surprises and real insight. The movement of the sermon is necessarily inductive, from life-as-lived to the text and back again. Aristotelian outlines can make this all but impossible, since deduction violates common sense, announcing conclusions ahead of the development of arguments and giving answers ahead of questions.[2] However disconcerting it may be, the Gospel cannot be captured by three points and a joke, anymore than life itself can be stuffed into that rhetorical corset.

There are obvious risks to preaching in new ways, but giving up control is one of life's most persistent tests of faith. For the listener to say a genuine "yes," she must have room to say a genuine "no." And self-persuasion asks that preachers stop blaming listeners for being so dull. Failure to be heard is more often than not a failure of words that are not worth hearing. Chances are they are not worth hearing because the one who speaks them has quit listening.

"Preaching, like singing, begins in the ear . . . and sermons are not just for saying what people want to hear, but for preaching what people want to say," Fred Craddock has reminded us.[3] How better to regard the ears of others than to begin with a regard for one's own? How best to have the last word but to make sure that the preacher is not the one who speaks it?

When children plead with parents to stop preaching at them, it is a request for less monologue, more dialogue, fewer clichés, more conversation. Don't the grown-ups in the pews deserve as much—a break from "ought," "must," and "should?" There are times when the preacher has every right to declare, to pronounce, even to thunder without equivocation. But exclamation marks ought to come at the end of confessions, not at the beginning of expositions. Ideally, it is the listener who punctuates.

Preaching as self-persuasion regards the listener as the dominant partner in the persuasion process. In fact, the listeners must participate in the sermon before it is written, speaking to the minister before the minister speaks to them. This requires a highly developed empathetic imagination, and though not every preacher has one, every preacher needs one. Fred Craddock suggests a simple exercise designed to keep in mind those for whom the sermon is written:

> Take a blank sheet of paper and write at the top "What's It Like to Be?" Beneath that heading, write a phrase descriptive of one concrete facet of human experience. Examples might be: "facing surgery," "living alone," "suddenly wealthy," "rejected by a sorority," "arrested for burglary," "going into the military," "fired from one's position," "graduating," "getting one's own apartment," "unable to read," "extremely poor," "fourteen years old." For the next fifteen minutes scribble on the page every thought, recollection, feeling, experience, name, place, smell, or taste that comes to mind.[4]

The result of this exercise is that ministers will discover, to their surprise, how much they really know about the human condition—even about those situations with which they have no personal experience. The power that is released in a sanctuary when those listening believe they are understood—by the Gospel, by the minister, and by God—is difficult to understate. It is this recognition on the part of the listener that the sermon is not just for them but about them that compels people to call such moments "relevant," "appropriate," or "just so personal." Preaching as self-persuasion can help to make such empathy possible, but first an enormous obstacle must be overcome.

Appetite before Insight

The word *grace* may be the most misunderstood word in Christendom. As a theological concept it is confusing, but as a facet of the sermon experience it is even less well understood. *Grace* has been defined as that mysterious provision by which God meets human need, always in measure beyond our deserving. But grace can by nature fill only empty space. In other words, it presumes appetite: "Blessed are those who hunger and thirst for righteousness, for they will be filled" (Matt. 5:6).

When it comes to religious insight, the listener who comes to the sermon without hunger will in a paradoxical sense always be hungry. Kierkegaard provides a striking metaphor for the church-goer who believes he has already heard everything the Gospel has to say and is now sitting before the pulpit out of habit, guilt, or the need for social acceptance. He compares such a listener to a man growing thinner day by day. The doctor explains to his family that the condition is not due to starvation but to eating all the time when not hungry and thereby ruining his digestion to the point that he resembles a starving man.

Preaching as self-persuasion assumes that listeners have come into the sanctuary expecting to *do* something, not just to *hear* something. But this is not the normal posture, especially for those who have grown up in the church. They hear the melodies of the church, and are comforted, but the meaning of the lyrics gets lost. People are frequently amazed to discover what good and bad theology is contained in the words of the hymns they sing every Sunday—words that have seldom been lifted out for examination apart from the obfuscating garb of a sentimental sound. Mouthed as increments of melody, they fail to register as vision, as indictment, or as stubborn hope. What is worse, the profound emotions that led the composer to take up the pen in the first place fade and eventually disappear, sacrificed on the altar of familiarity.

This is not to say that the familiar is without power. On the contrary, the Scriptures offer abundant evidence that it is in hearing anew what people thought they had already heard or learning afresh what they thought they already knew that makes a sermon both powerful and dangerous. When Jesus preached his first sermon in the synagogue of his home town, the reception was anything but cordial. It almost cost him his life (Luke 4:16–30). And not because he had invented some new gospel but because he used his community's own scripture to indict its behavior. Martin Luther King, Jr., did not conjure up some new manifesto for African Americans; he merely quoted from the Constitution we all share, taking as his text those words we had already enshrined but to which our pledge of allegiance was hypocritical.

Nevertheless, every preacher must confront the fact that listeners settle in at sermon time, saying "Here we go again." This is true not only because so much preaching is so utterly predictable, but because there is no expectation on the part of the listener that the sermon has a purpose other than the transfer of information. To consider it a catalyst, or a rhetorical experience whose very purpose is continued conversation, is as foreign a notion as that the preacher will be persuaded by his or her own sermon.

There are two possible responses to this malaise: to lament it or to change it. Lamentation can sometimes feel good and provide tender ministerial egos with a guilt-free diversion. But blaming the listener is a lot like that tired cliché about "putting Christ back in Christmas." After the vaguely satisfying feeling that comes from having lamented the vanishing breed of truly spiritual people in the world, nothing changes.

On the other hand, it is much riskier to suggest that the holiday be recovered through a reformation of behavior: limiting the gifts, outlawing debt as a means to express joy, and instituting domestic traditions like Scripture reading, candle lighting, or caroling at the nursing home. Otherwise we do not move beyond a kind of immobilized pity: "Isn't it awful!"

If the preacher inherits a congregation whose listening habits are deplorable, is that the same thing as saying that he has no power, over time, to create better listeners and a better listening environment? Instead of merely throwing a bag full of words into the air above the heads of the congregation, hoping some will fall with such a thud that they awaken those who have fallen asleep in the Gospel, perhaps he should take more responsibility for preparing ears as well as for preparing words. He can do this by making of himself not only a model speaker but a model listener as well.

To preach as if trying to persuade oneself is potent medicine for the listener precisely because it violates expectations. The last person in the house who is supposed to need Christian persuasion is the preacher. After all, this is the one paid to believe it, and paid to dispense it. This is the one who works on the sermon in the study ahead of time in order to arrive at answers to be delivered just in time. Having worked through the problem, the preacher may think she has only to stand and effectively deliver the solution. Why should she be surprised at anything she hears herself say?

Imagine what might happen to the pulpit if preachers came to it with an appetite, an expectation, a hunger to be moved in conversation with the Gospel. What if they expected to be angered, aroused, saddened, delighted, shaken, humored, and even dumbfounded by hearing the words they speak—even the words they know ahead of time they will speak?

Kenneth Burke said once, "You persuade a man only insofar as you can talk his language by speech, gestures, tonality, order, image, attitude, idea, identifying your ways with his."[5] In the case of preaching as self-persuasion, a sort of reverse identification takes place. The preacher models the listening behavior that is desired from the congregation, hoping to make it contagious. Over time, a self-persuading preacher's appetite for the Gospel becomes, by contagious example, the congregation's appetite for the Gospel.

If the preacher expects something to happen and manifests this expectation in voice, movement, and demeanor the congregation also begins to expect something to happen—after all, they don't want to be left out. They may have come to church with low expectations, but the preacher overcomes them by demonstrating high expectations. He opens the Bible to read as if turned loose in the attic of his great, great grandparent's house, excited to discover how little the passing years have changed the human condition. Here is a piece of verse, tender with love; here is a recipe, marking the needs of everyday life; here is the poetry of longing, of troubled questions, of hopeful answers.

He will hold the text in his mouth as if the wisdom of the ages was at stake, as if the words were hot with a life of their own. He will not kill the Scripture by mumbling syllables or stringing sentences together that have sound but no meaning. He will not walk to the pulpit as if to do his duty, but as if to do a number on himself. Gradually, almost imperceptibly, those who watch and listen begin to wonder, not what will he say, but what has he found in that common store that can still create such anticipation in the storekeeper. He acts as if he is about to cast a spell and wants to be the first to fall under it.

The Speaker as Listener

If preaching is to be relevant, it must also be appropriate. One of the most difficult tasks in the ministry of preaching is trying to decide, week after week, whether or not sermon material fits, whether it accomplishes that delicate negotiation of distance and intimacy so crucial to effective human communication. Although it is common to think of ministry as consisting of what is true and false, right and wrong, moral and immoral, the truth is that many of our most important decisions revolve around determinations of what is and what is not *appropriate*.

We have all been the unfortunate victims of the rhetorically inappropriate—the vulgar, painfully mismatched message and moment. Sometimes preachers who wish to be relevant accomplish little more than being hip: "Jesus and the boys were whooping it up one day down by the Sea of Galilee" is heard once too often the first time it's heard. Relevance is not manufactured but embodied, and one of the surest ways to determine appropriate language is for the speaker to try it out first against his own ear.

This does not require some sort of out-of-body experience but the simple yet rarely accomplished skill of speaking and listening simultaneously. It is the art of both turning words loose and being immediately affected by them, almost as if one were hearing them for the first time. The speaker listens, not like a speaker but like an audience. This "self-monitored" speech is governed by one overriding concern: what is the appropriate listener response?

If something is confused or obscure, the preacher ought to be the first to hear it, interrupting himself to apologize and try for a simpler phrase. If a sentence lacks clarity and concreteness, the preacher ought to be the first one disappointed. If a word no longer communicates to the modern ear, the preacher will translate it for his own sake, not just for the sake of being relevant. After all, his ear is modern! It is not selfishness that drives the self-persuading preacher to make his rhetoric worth his own time. It is the shortest route to the appropriate.

Self-monitored speech is not some rare new discovery. It is present in everyday discourse. What we call the ad lib is a result of speaking and listening simultaneously. The storyteller's embellishments, the actor's asides—they are not all that mysterious. They are the result of speakers who listen to themselves as carefully as they hope their audience will. They know when something is working, and when it isn't. So they edit in midsentence that communication may be served.

Think how common it is to hear even informal conversation interrupted with "to make a long story short . . ." or "to get to the heart of the matter . . ." or "a simpler way to put this might be . . ." What could cause each of these impromptu lines? The first might be a speaker who has heard herself drag a narrative out beyond the limits of her own patience; the second, a professor who senses too much extraneous material is clouding essential information because he is listening as a student might who is eager to commit a single phrase to memory; the third, a parent who tries to explain something to a child and realizes that the words overheard are not childlike enough.

We correct our speech constantly, not only because we sense impatience, discomfort, or confusion on the part of our listeners, but because we are also listening with feeling. And *our* ears are remarkably like those for whom our words are intended. The self-persuading preacher knows that what she spares her own ear, she spares every ear in the house. Consider for a moment how important this would be in those occasions of ministry where the appropriate is fundamental.

A wedding ceremony would never become the occasion for preaching a sermon on the evils of fornication; a funeral would never become the occasion for warning people of the dangers of not getting right with God soon enough; and Sunday morning would never be the occasion for scolding or putting down or lambasting the sinner. Why? Because the preacher would hear the deadly, hollow sound of his own words—words from which he had obviously exempted himself. Sometimes the rhetorically inappropriate constitutes a crime against humanity. Those who can't hear themselves can hardly expect to be heard.

Chapter 4
Self-Persuasion and Scripture

Our problem is to find a model that will liberate us from being fenced in by original meaning and yet, at the same time, relate us to an original meaning.

—David Buttrick

Overhearing the Gospel

One of the simplest and yet most profound things that can be said about the Bible is that not a single word of it is written to any one of us. Despite the oft-heard ranting, "The Bible says this" or "The Bible says that," the truth is that there is nothing in the Bible that addresses us directly. Canonization does not alter communicative form. It was all written by someone else, to someone else, and for purposes about which we can only make inference. This book, which is really an anthology of books written over thousands of years in multiple tongues and cultures, does not simply *say* something. What it may say to us is dependent upon our interpretations of what it once said.

It is little wonder that the Bible often baffles people who actually try to read it. All the tools of higher criticism must be employed for the purpose of positioning the reader on his knees, as it were, with ears cocked at a keyhole, listening to ancient conversations not intended for him. The case for "overhearing the gospel" has been made elsewhere,[1] and its impact on hermeneutics is far-reaching. What concerns us here is how the preacher who overhears the Gospel might also overhear the sermon.

Nevertheless, the posture of overhearing is so crucial to both hearing and speaking that it deserves a moment's review. Overhearing asks that first the preacher listen, because until the preacher has heard something, the preacher has nothing to say. Self-persuasion requires that we listen *before* we speak and then listen *as* we speak. To do this requires an understanding of the difference between exegesis and hermeneutics. The former, a transliterated Greek word with the verb form *exegeomai*, means "to tell about or recount—to bring out the meaning of something."[2] Exegesis has mostly to do with recovering the author's original meaning, as well as the meaning discerned by those who first read or heard the text. In short, what the text *meant*.

Hermeneutics, on the other hand, has to do with what the text *means*. It is preoccupied with the move from what a text *said* to what a text *says*. It is the process by which we ask: what present-day meaning is contained in this ancient text? Do we interpret the Bible or does the Bible interpret us? Is it possible to hear objectively, or do subjective factors always interfere with our ability to interpret any human utterance?

Although the difference between exegesis and hermeneutics is often debated and the lines are not clearly drawn, the preacher who wishes to be grounded in the text must be concerned with the polarity of meaning-then and meaning-now. Or is it the other way around, as James Smart has suggested? He writes of the distinction "between the meaning then and the meaning now as a treacherous one. The scholar . . . has no access to the original meaning unless the text has some meaning for him now."[3]

What must be avoided is a simplistic division of then and now, said and says, meant and means. To hear some preachers tell it, their sermon preparation is marked by two distinct halves. Like a machete dropped on a ripe watermelon, everything historical is lopped off on one side, and everything contemporary and relevant rolls the other way. Often the only connection between the two in the sermon is a hapless, "What this means for us today."

We have returned to a familiar dilemma: how much distance must be maintained from the text at the risk of losing intimacy, and at what point does intimacy begin to compromise the distance that objectivity requires? We cannot hang the whole meaning of the Gospel on the slender thread of the preacher's psyche. On the other hand, pretending that Scripture is self-authenticating because it is the Word of God violates the basic tenets of communication theory, not to mention common sense.

Preachers have negotiated this hermeneutical leap in various ways but often without adequate sensitivity to the tension we are describing. Some have claimed that there are perennial truths disguised by unfamiliar dress, and that all we have to do is change the wardrobe. This "kernel-within-the-shell" theory insists that the Word of God is equal to a distillation of propositional truth hiding in ancient and unfamiliar shells. The problem with such "extraction hermeneutics" is that it ignores basic realities of meaning: content cannot be totally separated from language, and things get not only lost in translation but altered as well.[4]

Preaching as self-persuasion offers a perspective that is helpful in the difficult task of interpretation. It does not offer a shortcut, for in preaching there are none. But it does suggest a posture—that of overhearing. Listeners are not to be made to feel like first-century Jews (any more than the preacher wishes to feel like one), nor is the rich legacy of biblical images and language to be sacrificed on the altar of modernism. Rather, the preacher is to use the tools of higher criticism to position herself to listen and to hear, as nearly as possible, the way those did who first heard. Ezekiel understood this when he said, "I came to the exiles at Tel-abib, who lived by the river of Chebar. And I sat there among them, stunned, for seven days" (Ezek. 3:15).

To overhear is to listen emphatically through exegesis. The experience is akin to sitting close enough to strangers in a restaurant to overhear much of the conversation. By the end of the evening, one is often unable to resist speculating on the occasion ("sounded like an anniversary to me"), the relationship ("newly married and still rather giddy"), the emotions ("an almost juvenile euphoria"), and the future ("Do you think they'll last?").

What makes overhearing such a powerful and appropriate tool for interpretation is that it maintains those two essential ingredients of hermeneutics: distance and intimacy. To have confronted the couple in the restaurant would have changed the nature of the experience completely. And yet preachers often confront the text, demanding that it offer up something utilitarian, something that "will preach." What they go looking for is usually what they find, because instead of maneuvering themselves into a position to listen, they move in on the text, hunting for evidence. Unfortunately, Scripture does not seem to speak clearly when held tightly by the throat.

Beyond this, self-persuasion suggests that communication happens most fully when listeners respond with relevant, self-generated messages. First the preacher is an empathic listener, so that he can be a listening speaker, so that his listeners can speak! The whole process is indirect and existential, but then so is Scripture. It is not a supermarket of propositional red meat, a warehouse of proof texts and illustrations for use in constructing legal briefs on eternal verities. It is a scrapbook of sacred memories, remnants of prophecy, snippets of verse, and reams of poetry. When read aloud, it was meant to save the Jewish and Christian community from spiritual amnesia.

Orality gave way to textuality only for practical reasons, to preserve the teachings and to create the Torah. But not because faith comes by reading. In a sense, the process of canonization was a process of preserving that material considered most self-persuasive. That is, when *this* story is told, when *this* poem is recited, when *this* prophetic warning is sounded, the people will respond with self-persuasive messages of affirmation: "That is indeed who we are" (children of Abraham); "This is indeed our joy and sorrow" (Job); "That is exactly how it feels to be frightened about the resurrection" (three women on Easter morning).

To overhear Scripture is to get close enough to an encounter with God to feel the contagious nature of its decisive and formative passion. Preaching as self-persuasion is almost like a form of public gossip—not for manipulating secrets but for the sake of reconstructing an encounter too important to keep quiet about. To overhear the self-persuasion preserved in Scripture is to gain insight into how the conversations of faith should sound. The relationship between a self-persuading preacher and a self-persuading congregation will be identical. Both will take their clue from what they overhear, and then both will be persuaded by what they are compelled to put into their own words.

The Remythologizing Ear

Rudolph Bultmann has suggested that the mythological structure of Scripture presents one of the most formidable hermeneutical tasks, that of "demythologizing" the text.[5] This requires a stripping away of prescientific, mythological wrappings that shroud perennial, existential truths. The assumption, much like the kernel-in-the-shell theory, is that the gift remains the same, regardless of the wrapping, and that a preacher's job is akin to unwrapping through exegesis what can then be rewrapped in more modern paper—perhaps with a few brightly colored bows as illustrations.

The problem with this approach, as we have already mentioned, is that it ignores some basic realities concerning the inseparability of form and content. Ernst Cassier makes a convincing case that language influences how we perceive, and what we perceive may influence our language. This is especially true of mythology. Suzanne Langer has described myth as primitive, nonlogical, and value-centered, expressing life, power, violence, evil, and death. It is language that is emotionally charged, not intending to convey understanding so much as identification among the people of a culture: "Mythic symbols do not even appear to be symbols; they appear as holy objects or places or beings, and their import is felt as inherent power."[6]

If we may stay with the analogy of a gift wrapped in cultural and cosmological paper, it becomes more difficult, given Langer's view, to artificially separate one from the other. The experience of the truth of Scripture is inextricably woven into the listener's experience of the text. To discard the wrapping is also, partly at least, to discard the gift.

The self-persuading preacher must therefore be on guard against the archaic but not necessarily against the mythical. The Bible is full of universal archetypal images that transcend culture and language: bread, shared meals, seeds, lost sons, dying children, aged parents with cloudy eyes, and pain as vivid as a spear thrust into the side of a dying man. If demythologizing means draining the text, vampirelike, of its very passion, then we have thrown out the baby with the bath water.

In this regard, the self-persuading preacher has a simple but profoundly important tool at her disposal: her own ear. Shaped by the sound and sense of this life, not some other, it is the same ear as that belonging to her listeners. Never mind that she has acquired some special vocabulary in seminary—most of it is useless for preaching. If she desires to communicate, she will speak of end times, not matters "eschatalogical." She will speak of a new life in Christ, not of "soteriology." And she will speak of the complicated business of interpreting Scripture, not of the "hermeneutical circle." Specialized words have their place, but think how much more communication would occur if people would just say "type" instead of "genre."

The self-persuading preacher submits the text to his own ear first on behalf of his "like-eared" congregation, not to spare them from mythology but to *remythologize* it. The cult of gluttony as a means to happiness was described one way by Paul, but now the cult of starvation and compensatory materialism is described another way: "You can't be too rich or too thin." People haven't stopped living by myths. Some of the myths have simply gotten grotesque.

Remythologizing is a reconstructing activity, not an apologetic one. The self-persuading preacher listens not just for what is true, but for *how* something is true. And the Bible itself gives vivid instruction in how the community of faith talks to itself. Hearing in one form, the self-persuading preacher does not preach in another. For not only would this be intellectually dishonest, but it would deprive the listeners (of which she is one) of the opportunity to catch what the preacher is supposed to be making contagious: an experience of the truth.

In order to remythologize, one must respect the power of indirect communication and also responsibly translate biblical content into the idioms of the day. Self-persuading preachers will not go looking for lessons or points but will listen for words that stir the imagination and excite the senses. The sensual language of theological drama will not be edited out as intellectually suspect or academically shallow. After all, without passion there is no persuasion:

> Have you ever sat on a Sunday morning before the reading of some rich text, moved by the ancient imagery: hills skipping like lambs; the earth shaking under the heavy foot of the Almighty walking up to Jerusalem from Sinai; God with a long white beard; a valley of dry bones; a tender sprout on an old stump; Satan plaguing the solitude of Jesus in the fierce desert; Paul caught up to the third heaven; streets of gold and a chorus of white robed saints? Soon kindred images, some sober, some foolish, are spawned in the listener's stirred mind. Then the preacher arises to "explain" all the images to the "modern mind." What is offered is really a disguised apology for the poor ancient writer.[7]

The self-persuading preacher overhears the Gospel not only to discover that certain words no longer communicate to the modern ear, but also to discover that some still do. In order to make the distinction, the preacher must do something very important before a single word of the sermon is written: read the text aloud and pronounce the text properly. If there is to be any meaning communicated through listening, then the preacher is responsible for the inflections that distinguish that meaning. This means more than simply being correct. It means the text must be performed and experienced, speaking as one might imagine the original speaker did and listening as one might imagine the original listener did.

It is here that the theoretical aspects of self-persuasion take on a very practical tone. Speaking to listen and listening to speak, the preacher must first experience the text acoustically, allowing the words to create a circle that first echoes emotions and then elicits them. In the human drama of Scripture, fear has a sound, high and tight; so does longing; it is tired and drawn out. Awe and wonder have a sound too—it is a paradoxical sound, like trying to shout what can only be whispered. The *sound* of Scripture matters ultimately to the self-persuading preacher, because until he has heard what to feel, he cannot speak with enough feeling to be heard.

The process of self-persuasion begins in the ear and is completed by the compulsion to speak. The speaking brings a new hearing and effects subsequent speech. It is almost impossible to determine where one ends and the other begins, but this much is certain: the acoustics of delivery are dependent upon the acoustics of conception. A sermon not spawned by the ear may be stillborn on the tongue. Listen, then speak, then listen to yourself speaking.

Read the text as if you were reading for the theater. Bestow upon words the blessed inequity that conversational tone requires: shrink the articles, employ contractions for haste, and linger on names, savoring the sound. A single word can launch a whole sermon, if you read and listen with feeling. But do not assume that you can find the germinal idea for your sermon by putting on your spectacles alone. You've also got to clear your throat.

Interpretation as Conversation

The process of understanding and being understood is a lifelong dialectic rooted in language. When meaningful talk dies, the human spirit begins to die. There is ample research to verify that when communication ceases, so does emotional health, physical health, even life span.[8] There is no need to explain this to ministers, however. They notice how quickly the death of one spouse often follows the funeral of the other.

Oddly enough, if a preacher is to have a life-sustaining and renewable relationship with Scripture, then he is going to have to converse with it. As a reference tool, the Bible quickly loses any spark that might ignite a sermon worth hearing. But as a conversation partner, the possibilities are endless. What is more, the passion we seek is in this exchange. When Martin Buber talks of I-Thou, he isn't referring to the preacher and the Bible. But for the self-persuading preacher, the model works, the metaphor fits.

In a sense, sermons are born in soliloquy; they germinate whenever the silence between the preacher and the text is broken. R. E. C. Browne once wrote: "He [the preacher] must work in solitude to achieve a personal form of speech, which though clearly his own, calls attention not to himself but to the many-sidedness of the truth of the Gospel."[9] To work in solitude, however, does not necessarily mean to work quietly. A preacher who is disciplined enough to perform the text, overhear it, and then converse with it is someone to be heard with profit. The study door ought to be shut, however, and not just for privacy. Rather, so that the self-persuading preacher may speak aloud, and with feeling, without having to offer repeated assurances of sanity to the church staff.

It is in solitude that the preacher first tries out the sound of the text in conversation with the sound of herself. She questions, argues, teases, postulates, paraphrases, mimics, cajoles, compliments, interrogates, and complicates. She is searching for a *point of contact*, something that will quicken the imagination, and prompt a conversation worth having and worth hearing. Kierkegaard reminds us that the highest form of communication is not the transfer of information but the creation of an experience through which the listeners feel obligated.

Jesus of Nazareth understood how tired and flat words could become—how empty and like mere incantation is the sound of teaching disconnected from teachers. Scripture as authoritative monologue is an illusion, and that is why it was standard for the Galilean to begin by saying, "You have heard it *said* . . . but I *say* . . ." (see Matthew 5). The Law is only complete in conversation with real life. Furthermore, it is never static but always in search of an argument worthy of clarifying it, a conversation partner bold enough to fashion, for the sake of its essence, a new hearing.

We sometimes speak as if the Bible can be considered the Word of God just as it lies on the page, static and lifeless. If this were the case, we should pass out pieces of paper containing the text for the day, allow sufficient time for reading, and then dismiss the faithful in silence. But the fact is we need to hear the text engaged, amplified, and turned loose in a new form. That means the preacher must talk as honestly with his congregation as he talks with himself.

There is evidence to suggest that when people talk to themselves, they are candid and cryptic. We apparently do not waste words on ourselves; we do not exaggerate or deceive, and we have no tolerance for puffed-up, bloated rhetoric. With ourselves, we get down to the point. After all, who would we be trying to fool?

Unfortunately, when preparing a speech or sermon, we become grandiose, abstract, and long-winded. None of the first private reactions to the text, mumbled in the privacy of the study, make it into the pulpit. "So what has the exorcism of this epileptic demon got to do with my temptation to commit adultery?" Too bad. Everyone would be listening from that moment on.

People are hungry to hear the church's wisdom engaged in lively and meaningful conversation. They know the text is not written for them, but they sense that the words are written about them. They are looking for more than the point of the parable. They are looking for the experience of being interpreted by the parable. And they want to know if something has touched the minister so deeply she can't keep quiet about it. Perhaps she will jump-start their conversation, and the text will live again.

For the self-persuading preacher, this means that the first reading, the performance of the text in the study, will come before a single commentary is consulted. Before reading what the experts claim to be the meaning of the text, the words of it will have a chance to make their own first impression. As much as possible, proper rhetorical punctuation should be used, so that a question actually sounds like a question, an exhortation like an exhortation, and a blessing like a blessing. Remember, a text not only says something, it does something.

When commentaries are consulted, when words are translated, and when authorship, intention, and context are better understood, a whole new hearing may take place. But the preacher must remember that the way she hears the text the first time is the only way her audience will ever hear it. There are no Greek and Hebrew lexicons in the pews. Most people will not even bother to look the passage up and read along. It is all a kind of scriptural Musak to them, an elevator-music prelude to the main event. In fact, Scripture is often read with so little energy, so little vocal variety and emphasis that it sounds almost like an ecclesiastical disclaimer—something that is droned through to sanctify the real words that follow. In communication, as with coronary care, a flat line says the heart isn't doing well.

A preacher who does not listen to himself read the text will not listen to himself preach either. And a congregation that does not hear passion in the Scripture can hardly expect the sermon to become its passionate conversation partner. This passion cannot be faked, of course, or we get a talking head. But it can be heard in the voice—expectation, intensity, respect—and seen in the body language, a posture of discovery. In the way the pages are turned (don't have the Bible already marked), the congregation can feel an eagerness. In the face, eyes, and hands, there is communicated one of two things: either the preacher looks forward to the experience of the sermon, anxious to amplify and sanctify the conversation, or he is just getting through it, worn down by mouthing words he can hear but has long ago ceased listening to.

Perhaps an example here would serve to amplify a very subtle theoretical concept. A first reading of that fascinating story in Genesis 32 where Jacob wrestles all night with an angel can be experienced at many different levels as one's study of the text unfolds. But the *first* reading may render some of the most relevant responses. Although the modern ear may be confused by talk of river demons and the hiddenness of God, there is an immediate and profound reaction to Jacob's paranoia, his fear of returning home to face an older brother from whom he stole a blessing, and the crude tactics of appeasement whereby even within families people try to buy each other's love and forgiveness.

Even before scholars have explained a single facet of the text and thereby turned yet more passion loose on the ear, the first reading of this patriarchal tale brings a simple but extraordinarily important line to the center of consciousness. On the night of Jacob's strange encounter with what he thinks is an angel but turns out to be God at work, wounding his old self in the mortal combat of conscience, we read: "That same night he got up and took his two wives, his two maids, and his eleven children, and crossed the ford of the Jab'bok. He took them and sent them across the stream, and likewise everything that he had. Jacob was left alone" (Gen. 32:22–24a).

It is that final word, capturing as it does a condition unfamiliar to Jacob, that acts like a magnet for the entire story—a germinal idea whose relevance in human experience transcends the ages. He was left *alone*. A man who normally travels with an entourage the size of a small village, and has every pacifying gadget that money can buy is suddenly alone at the edge of a river. Alone with his fear, his guilt, and whatever may go bump in the night. The solitude had not been self-sought; that could have been intentional therapy. He is *left* alone. Alone to face the spirit of One who can be neither deceived nor purchased. But by the time the sun comes up, he is both renamed and walking with a limp. Israel is his name, the nation that is wounded by wrestling with God.

From the very first reading of the text, one simple word, *alone*, sets off a string of images and associations that shape the sermon as a continuing conversation. What was heard is not just ancient history or doctrine in disguise but the sound of the human condition. The experience is one of both distance and intimacy, which in the final analysis is the only approach to Scripture that works. We perform the text in order to overhear it. Overhearing it gets us talking to ourselves and listening in on this new conversation engages and commits us at a deeply personal level. Going public with this conversation is risky, but the reward is great: we may not only persuade ourselves, but facilitate the self-persuasion of others.

Chapter 5
Self-Persuasion and the Nature of Authority

I have found words for my inmost thoughts, songs for my joy, utterances for my hidden griefs, and pleadings for my shame and feebleness. In short, whatever finds me bears witness for itself that it has proceeded from the Holy Spirit.

—Samuel Coleridge

Listening to Me, Myself, and I

Self-persuasion theory rests on one very simple but central premise: the messages we generate for ourselves are more authoritative than those from an outside source. This clear and decisive break with classical rhetoric locates persuasion at the ear of the listener, not at the mouth of the rhetor. And there exists a substantial body of research to back up the claim that when it comes to authority, the holiest of trinities is Me, Myself, and I.

Experiments have shown that whenever someone is personally involved with an attitude, idea, or issue—made to own it by virtue of investing in its espousal or defense—there is a clear movement toward adoption of the attitude, idea, or issue. Some of the earliest experiments involved simply asking subjects to write their own argument for something and comparing the extent of their persuasion to those who merely read an argument written by someone else. The findings indicate that the persistence of opinion change was positively correlated to active involvement, and that the authors had superior recall of the topic and the argument supported.[1]

In 1959, Festinger and Carlsmith published their then startling findings that individuals who, for a one-dollar bribe, told a person that a dull task was actually interesting were more likely to believe it than did those who told the same lie for a twenty-dollar bribe. Less "dissonance" was created when a larger sum of money was paid because the greater sum justified the deception. When the monetary inducement was all but absent, the subject had to invest more of himself in the reduction of the dissonance and hence came to believe the lie in order to justify telling it. An external force created an internal adjustment: twenty dollars "bought" the lie; but one dollar couldn't. So the "underpaid" persuaded themselves that it wasn't a lie after all.

All of this makes sense at the intuitive level, but it is impressive to note how often social scientific research confirms notions about self-persuasion. Examples from everyday life prove that when there is a need to adopt a certain attitude or belief based on self-interest, people can be very convincing. When stuck in a dismal marriage or a dead-end job, people often construct elaborate and quite impressive lists of reasons for sticking with both. These rationales have been rehearsed aloud many times in order that the most important person of all will be persuaded by them.

Role-playing also demonstrates the transforming effects of the self interacting with itself. When subjects were asked to encode what are called "belief-discrepant messages," they showed significantly more attitude change when they role-played than when they did not.[2] The old actor's adage applies: to act the part, one must become the part. If an actor fails to self-persuade, the lines she delivers will have a distinctly hollow sound. The acting coach will always offer the same counsel: listen to yourself deliver the lines until it is not yourself that you hear but the character you have become. Talented actors do this so well that if the show runs for months or even years, they can experience an eerie confusion about their identity. They are not always sure which person they are, and they find themselves talking like their character in settings outside the theater. After all, we are known by the company we keep.

The implications of this phenomenon for preaching fairly jump off the page. Just as we listen for the sound of a text and judge its power and significance against our own ear, so too are the words we speak to be judged by the authentic or unauthentic sounds we make. How honest is our speech? How genuine and relevant? How pious and hollow? As preachers, we are not paid to move our mouths and make religious sounds. We are paid to struggle on behalf of our congregation to *reconcile* the sounds of faith with the character of the faithful—including ourselves. If no disparity is perceived and no real dissonance is created, the resulting sound is likely to be hollow indeed, not to mention self-righteous.

The self-persuading preacher does not just listen for the sound of the text and duplicate it. He listens for the authentic sound of his own conversation. If he isn't in character, the sound will be unmistakable. If he has gone looking for simple platitudes, the voice will be in concert; if he is angry and looking for spiritual ammunition, the vocal cords will lead the march; but if he is confused or amazed, curious or inspired, the real symphony will begin, and a melody line for the sermon will take shape.

Remember, the preacher is not in the business of reporting to a congregation what a text *said*. The self-persuading preacher is in the business of creating an experience in which the text *says* something. What hasn't been heard can't be transposed, and what is out of tune will be painful for everyone. There is a reason why we don't let musicians without a good ear loose on the stage; the same should apply to preachers. What has not been tuned in private should never be performed in public. Harmony has an existential as well as a tonal quality. Next to bad theology, the leading cause of bad preaching is deafness.

If Daryl Bem is correct and people infer their beliefs to some degree from their behavior,[3] then preaching as self-persuasion becomes a sort of test. The preacher asks: Since I am always talking about being a Christian, does that mean I am one? If language really is performative, then my words can be thought of as deeds. If I listen to myself, I should learn a great deal about the gap that separates behavior and attitude and feel the need to close it. In this sense, self-monitored speech becomes nothing short of therapeutic.

Again, the operating principle is that the self is the highest seat of authority, and that hearing ourselves talk about important and intimate things cannot help but produce change if the process is the least bit self-conscious. If there is dissonance, we will hear it first, and our language will sound confessional. If there is inspiration, we will hear it first, and our language will sound infused. If there is confusion, doubt, or anger, we will hear it first, and our language will quake and stumble. What we *feel* makes what we *hear* feel right. And feeling right about what we hear ourselves feeling becomes a kind of rhetorical spiral that joins sound, sense, and conviction in a crescendo of self-persuasion.

This is why someone else's words just won't do. Those who play games in the pulpit, claiming on a certain Sunday that they will "just let Paul do the talking," are involved in a double deception. First, because for all practical purposes, Paul can't do the talking. And second, because if he could, persuasion at the highest level would never take place. It would be like placing rhetorical tracing paper over the text and then holding up the copy as if it were art. Smiling and acting humble do not make forgery any less a crime. The self-persuading preacher must converse with the masters and then create originals. She must put the sermon in her own words. How else will she know what she really believes?

Appropriation, Authentication, Ownership

Tuning in carefully to the sound of the text and then to the sound of one's own voice in conversation with the text is not done just for the sake of harmony. The self-persuading preacher is also after a feeling, a distinctly personal experience that comes from grasping something as true and then having the true sound of it vibrate against both ear and heart. This is what Shelley called a "truth of the emotions." It is not that things are true because we say them, but it is true that when we say them, and believe them, they possess the only kind of authority that really matters.

The church may well have wasted the lion's share of its energy over the years trying to persuade people that the Bible, or the pope, or the creeds of the faith possess authority independent of any personal appropriation of their message. To be told that something is true is, in a sense, the antithesis of self-persuasion. All that such a declaration can do is raise an issue to the level of consciousness or perhaps make it plausible by virtue of the credibility of the messenger. But until the listener authenticates it in his own experience, grasps it as true, and articulates it through the creation of new, self-generated messages, there is no authority per se in the original message.

Granted, this sounds perilously close to total subjective existentialism, but the issue is not what is true but what has authority in the mind of the listener. Many things perceived to be true are in fact not true, and other things that are true may never be understood as such. But the process of persuasion is more than information processing or the transfer of cognition. It is an emotional event requiring insight seized *for* the self, *by* the self. And its principle manifestation is some sort of exclamation, followed by an irresistible desire to put the discovery into one's own words.

Upon dull ears fall the omnipresent premise: "The Bible says . . ." or "The Holy Father says . . ." or "Our Church teaches . . ." Blind submission to the external authority vested in institutions, objects, or persons is a kind of coercion that is to be differentiated from persuasion. Coercion masquerades as authority by threatening the uncooperative or disbelieving person with negative consequences. Saying "yes" means nothing unless saying "no" is a real possibility. Call it the falcon principle, if you will: the company of someone means a great deal more if she is free to leave, or having once left, comes back.

Preaching as self-persuasion is necessarily a kind of RSVP—response is kindly requested but nothing is guaranteed. The important thing is that the preacher not exempt himself from the very process by which his listeners will lay hold of ideas, adopt them, and speak them aloud. If he does, he takes away the self-persuading role model and perpetuates the myth that faith is a commodity, stored in the professional and doled out in increments to the customer. It would be better if he remembered what Browning said of Guido in *The Ring and the Book*: "So shall the truth be flashed out in one blow, and Guido see one instant and be saved."

In the classroom we call it the "Ah Ha!" experience, and it is almost always followed by an energy to articulate. The good teacher does not let that energy go unexpended: "Tell me what you understand now." Wordsworth used to seed his conversations with friends in a unique way. If he had not seen them for some time, he would begin: "Tell me what has come clear to you since last we met."

Insight does not leave articulation undisturbed; it compels it. And thoughts are not full-born until they are expressed. Expressing them creates a new experience, that of overhearing, and often a kind of chain-reaction is set off, light following upon light, insight tumbling over itself. Artists call this a "creative fit."

Why do people insist that learning at the highest level takes place when you have to teach the subject matter? Because a move from memorization to articulation is required. Explaining it makes it yet more clear, even to the explainer. The most memorable teachers are those who are moved by their own lectures.

In *Irrational Man: A Study in Existential Philosophy*, William Barrett points out that the Greek word for "I know," *oida*, is the perfect form of the verb "to see," and means "I have seen." "He who knows is the man who has seen."[4] The same idea is captured in the Latin phrase *Non foras ire, in interiore homine habitate veritas*. It means: "Go not without, for within man dwells the truth." When it comes to authority in religion, the heart must grasp, and then the lips must give utterance to that which is laid hold of.

It might be easy to argue that in matters more mundane than religion, self-persuasion need not occur. Experts tell us things that we accept on the strength of their expertise. The speed of light, for example, is something we trust the scientist to work out in the lab. But when it comes to matters of life and death, what Maslow calls "core values," we may be light years away from being persuaded to love our enemies. Kierkegaard reminded us, "Christianity is not a doctrine but an existential communication."[5]

The purpose of the sermon, according to the Danish philosopher, was not to fill the head with redemptive information but to fill the heart and soul with unrest and a feeling of obligation. Not an obligation to say "yes" or "no" to some doctrinal proposition, but an obligation to continue the conversation of the text within the listener's personal life. Preaching, to Kierkegaard, was the artful shifting of a burden from the preacher who struggles to the listener who must struggle. Any sermon entitled, "Shortcuts to Faith" is an exercise in deception.

The very word *religio*, from *re-ligare*, "to bind," means a link—a ligament—between the soul and God. In a sense, being in love with God.[6] So what faith can there be without the lover's quarrel? And since God does not talk back in the conventional sense, how is the believer to interact except through a sustained and sustaining intrapersonal dialectic?

In the movie *Fiddler on the Roof* the character of the father takes daily walks as an excuse to argue with God. He teases the silent sky with his questions, he shakes his fist at life's enigmas, and then he waits for the answers to come out of his own mouth. It was in listening to himself ask the questions that answers came. And it was in listening to himself speak the answers that resolution came.

Self-persuasion is a form of communication concerned first and last with the listener's response. This means that preaching must be in service to the experience of insight rather than to the admiration of itself as a rhetorical entity. A satisfied listener may say, "That was a good speech," meaning it could be delivered in a variety of contexts by a variety of speakers with predictable enjoyment. But the self-persuading preacher is after more than enjoyment. She is after dialectic. Her method is essential Socratic, and her object is to disturb the listener, not merely to edify.

When Augustine tries to answer the question of what makes good preaching, he begins by offering standard rhetorical advice. Then, piece by piece, he takes it back and treats what he has been saying as irrelevant, concluding: "God himself is the persuader in good preaching."[7] Why didn't Augustine just begin there? The answer lies in his method of arriving at truth. He leads the reader through an experience of considering and then rejecting a series of ideas, "as though bridges were being burned behind the traveler through the pages until finally all is consumed except the destination."[8] What we have in *On Christian Doctrine, Bk 4*, is the Bishop of Hippo talking to himself and inviting the reader to do the same. This is not so much rhetoric as midwifery. And it is essentially Platonic because the Preacher as Teacher often helps us to remember and reaffirm what we already know.

Saying "Amen!" The Power of Recognition

The African-American preaching tradition in America has taught us the most about self-persuasion. What is often characterized as "emotionalism," especially the sound of the listener saying "Amen!" is really indicative of just how inherently dialogical and overtly listener-centered the African-American preaching tradition is. What we chalk up to differences in the races has more to do with differences in communication strategy than with genetic propensities. The operating principle is this: the Gospel is community property. It belongs to everyone present to hear it. The preacher's role is to turn it loose, and the "amen" is a natural response to recognizing, with renewed urgency, what is already known.

It is also true that African-Americans do not share the Western schism of reason vs. feeling that is one of the sadder legacies of the Enlightenment. They have retained a "wholeness"—an interdependence of head and heart that is typical of many other cultures. Hence African-American preaching fuses content with experience and carries the communal nature of truth as both memory and insight into the festival-like atmosphere of African-American worship.[9] For our purposes, the musicality and dialogical nature of this tradition teach vitally important lessons about preaching as self-persuasion.

It is often assumed that the essence of good preaching is to tell people something that they never knew but always needed to know. But the most powerful kind of preaching occurs when a listener recognizes that what he already thought was true really is true. In the West, we tend to refer to this as an appeal to the subconscious. But Henry Mitchell, an African-American preacher, refers to it as the "transconscious." Tapping into this innate and universal religious sentiment requires a form of communication that teaches people new words to old songs:

> Far from being an avant-guard experiment, it is actually a return to a "primitive" sophistication about how faith is shared, nourished, and refined. Transconscious communication is a matter of using the mouth-to-ear methods that planted folk faith in the first place. Thus beliefs and trusts once transmitted by stories, until they were part of the deepest consciousness (usually misleadingly referred to as the unconscious), must be resurrected, pruned, and improved, or replaced to provide better tales for today. [10]

It is important for the preacher, of whatever background or tradition, to remember that those who sit before the pulpit have not come to hear a new story but to experience a new hearing of the Old Story. It is not for the breaking of new ground that they come but in the hope that someone can bring to fruition the lingering, if sometimes faint, feeling that the Word of God is *in* them. After all, "the point of religious language is . . . to stimulate the process of experience and thought which will reconstitute human personality."[11]

The word *reconstitute* deserves a closer look. It means, literally, "to constitute again, reconstruct, recompose." We do not start from scratch but alter what already exists. Theologians today are talking and writing about what has been called "Primal Memory"—the sense that we are *from* God, and *to* God, and that life itself is a brief parenthesis in which we struggle to remember where we came from, where we are going, and to whom we belong. The historian of religions Mircea Eliade calls it a universal "nostalgia" that underlies the creation of everything valuable in and of itself: art, the sciences, social theory, and "all the other things to which men will give the whole of themselves."[12]

Eliade suggests that worldviews are generated as the "result of immemorial existential situations," or what Mitchell calls "stored insight." In a sense, good preaching turns on the light in this collective basement, leading the worshippers down the stairs of memory into a room where together they can celebrate "transconsciousness." People are always amazed to discover how remarkably similar are the broad ethical imperatives and general teachings of the world religions. Why should we be surprised? It is a testimony to the universal activity of God in human affairs.

For the self-persuading preacher, the facilitation of memory is crucial not for learning the eight steps on the ladder of glory, but for tapping into shared religious insight and creating a reunion of sorts between God and his estranged creation. Remember, those who sit before the preacher are full of faulty assumptions about why their minister is preaching. They believe it is because he has something to hand over or hand out. He is the salesperson, they are the customers, and he had better be good because they are hard to sell, and money is tight, and they have heard this pitch before. What they don't expect and might be mesmerized to witness is a preacher who could compel them to converse by virtue of the example of his own conversing.

Preaching as self-persuasion takes identical human nature so much for granted that it proceeds almost like a rhetorical mime—where movements have meaning because so many are universal. This is what African-American preachers have understood since the days of slavery. One does not have to keep interrupting the sermon to ask whether the congregation "gets it," "understands what is meant," or "has ever felt this way." The preacher strikes the chord not by announcing it but by using the pitch pipe of human commonality. The listeners are not called upon to agree or disagree so much as to recognize and decide. Although Western culture tried to prove that the Scriptures were rational and the faith was practical, African-American preaching "has stated that which was logically irrefutable in ways which were artistically and existentially *irresistible*."[13]

The "Amen!" of African-American worship has its roots in West African communal celebrations, where Africans danced, sang, and told stories to explain and experience harvest, marriage, life, and death in such a way that everyone was involved. The language was "tonal," and so children grew up learning it almost subliminally. And although improvisation kept it interesting, the basic content (the transconscious melody) remained fixed. Everyone knew how the story went, and so no one dared to make a mistake. When Africans arrived on these shores, they came equipped to read the stories of the Bible as if they were but variations on the liberation stories of their youth. To new English subtitles, they brought the musicality and corporate participation of the feast at home.[14]

In African-American preaching, the sermon is not private property. The minister does not speak *to* the people but *for* them, and empathy need not be contrived, only embodied. The purpose of the sermon is to plead everyone's pleading, to exalt everyone's exaltation, and to talk so honestly about the life of faith that everyone's tongue is loosed. The preacher's compulsion to speak diminishes the congregation's hesitation to speak.

The real authority in preaching is located not in the truth of a particular utterance but in the recognition that once uttered, truth is no long particular. It belongs to the community of faith. The response may be "Amen!" or "Yes!" Or it may be a look on the face, a move to the edge of the pew, an unconscious movement of the lips. The preacher who understands that the most powerful inducement to self-persuasion is to engage in self-persuasion will not have to bait the audience. He will merely have to respect it and remember that nothing serves collective memory like individual honesty.

Chapter 6
Self-Persuasion and the Person of the Preacher

Never trust the teller, trust the tale.

—D. H. Lawrence

Intimacy and Distance

If only things were as simple as the novelist presumes. The truth is that in every rhetorical moment we respond to some*one*. The message and the messenger are inseparable. For centuries the church has debated the issue, with Augustine and Donatus squaring off early on: Is the efficacy of preaching contingent upon the faith and morals of the preacher, or are clergy, like other professionals, allowed to be "human" even as they traffic in things divine? Like all true dilemmas, it can be demonstrated that both positions are tenable. But to artificially separate the preacher's character and personality from the intimacy that is preaching is to ignore a powerful maxim in philosophy: *agere sequitur esse*. It means that one's actions follow from one's being. What one does or what one says follows from what one is.

The insight is hardly modern. Aristotle claimed that *ethos*, or the perceived characteristics of the speaker, constituted the most important ingredient in persuasion. Of the three kinds of proof in rhetoric, he wrote, the most authoritative is that "supplied by character."[1] Quintilian made the case even more clearly when he wrote that an orator, as defined by Marcus Cato, is "a good man, skilled in speaking."[2]

If the messenger is not believable, then neither is the message. A minister remembers the comment of a parishioner from a New

Jersey congregation on the occasion of hearing their beloved minister emeritus speak: "He is so loved . . . he could stand up and read his laundry list, and we would be moved to tears." Wittgenstein reminded us of what we all know intuitively, that the *character* of life out of which words come is inescapably involved in the meaning of those words, and Craddock applies this principle to preaching: "No one can increase the volume in the pulpit to such a level as to muffle the echo of lost convictions. Passion makes one persuasive."[3]

The reader has the right to raise a logical objection here, but we need to grant it and move on without apology. No one is claiming that the Gospel has no autonomy or objectivity apart from the character of the preacher. After all, we preach from words not written to us, and we recognize that the faith is inherited, not invented. But just as there was passion and inspiration involved in getting the words of Scripture *onto* the page, so must there be passion and inspiration in getting them *off* the page. There is a big difference, we all know, between a sermon and a lecture. The difference is in the speaker.

For some reason, discussions about the relationship between the person of the preacher and the effectiveness of the Gospel preached is troublesome to many religious professionals. It has become, in many homiletic circles, almost a taboo subject. But when those who listen to sermons are polled, it appears at the top of their list of concerns. And always, the word they use most is *trust*. The level of trust corresponds to the level of intimacy. And the level of intimacy dictates the freedom and security necessary to think about the Gospel, rather than about whether the minister is a hypocrite.

Psychiatrist Ronald Laing uses the expression "existential birth" to describe the foundation for the feeling of being a real person and the emergence of a fundamental or ontological security. In the womb, there were no problems for us. We did not have to decide whether we really wanted to live or not. Only when we experienced physiological independence, disinclination, hunger, misery, waiting, and anxiety for the first time, did we have to ask ourselves whether or not we wanted to affirm the life we had received.[4]

Once independent, the need for security is dominant, and the consequences of insecurity are continuous and disastrous. Erik Erikson coined the expression "primal trust" and used it to describe the cornerstone of the healthy personality.[5] The same primal trust must be developed in the relationship between the preacher and the congregation in order for the tenuous and complicated business of faith exploration and development to move forward. Without it, a myriad of dysfunctional attitudes and behaviors ensue: the preacher resents the listeners and scolds them; the listeners resent the preacher and tune her out; the sermon either drags through generalities or descends into navel-gazing. Every counselor knows that basic trust precedes meaningful communication. In preaching, the stakes are incredibly high.

For one thing, ministry is a profession unlike any other. If the practice of law and medicine often require a level of trust on the part of clients that goes far beyond what was learned in graduate school, consider the trust that must surround the pastoral relationship. For one thing, doctors and lawyers have the luxury of dealing with one person at a time. They do not have congregations; they have clients. Adjusting to an audience of one is a far simpler task than adjusting to an audience of many. And a whole lot less risky as well.

One word, one approach, one style cannot possibly be right for everyone. Yet ministers are supposed to speak the right word at the right time for the most important moments in people's lives. What does one say to a nervous young man and a nervous young woman who stand before the altar of marriage with a greater chance of failure than of success? What about the child taken into one's arms for baptism? His parents may not be "regular" at church but have come to "have him done." Surrounded by family and friends, cameras at the ready, is one to offer up some bland and ritual rhetoric, or is it better to talk of a helpless child, helpless parents, and the mystery of a formless tomorrow? Are we nervous because the baby might spit up on us, or are we all afraid that parenthood is impossible without God's help?

Ministers may be kind, gentle, educated, well intentioned, law-abiding—you finish the list. But if they cannot negotiate distance and intimacy, then how are they supposed to say the right word at the right time? Clergy are asked to do something very difficult: maintain enough distance to be a leader and cultivate enough intimacy to be a pastor. They must stand back sometimes, for they represent ancient truth not to be compromised and an invisible God not to be made trivial. And yet they are also asked to be a flesh-and-blood model of what faith actually *does* to a person. For if they show no evidence of a life shaped in concrete ways by the Gospel, then how can they expect to preach about a life-changing Gospel?

People expect ministers to be both human and exceptional. They do not, however popular the excuse may be, expect them to be perfect. What people have the right to expect is that there is something about traffic with the Gospel that causes change in the practitioner of the Gospel. That change cannot help but find its way into speech, both in matters of form and content. R. E. C. Browne explains, when it comes to the exposition of doctrine:

> The speaker must constantly remember that he is part of the reality he discusses; in fact when he speaks of anything he is inevitably talking about himself, for he is not a spectator of the complexity he seeks to understand. Religion is not a way of mastering this complexity but of bearing it.[6]

Listeners have the right to know if their preacher has a calling that still excites her, compels her, and transforms her, or whether she is acting the part of Religious Master of Ceremonies. People are looking for a real person in the pulpit, but they want a better-than-average person. Someone who is not comfortable with this expectation should probably consider another line of work. In fact, it would be wise if no one entered the ministry unless it became impossible not to. For without such compulsion, parish ministry will overwhelm and destroy those without genuine spirituality, authentic compassion, and the capacity for personal renewal.

Preaching as self-persuasion offers help at many levels. First, the sensibilities that develop out of the relationship between the preacher and the text are the very same ones that govern the relationship between the preacher and the congregation: distance and intimacy. Second, the conversations with the text that are meant for and governed by the preacher's own ear are bound to be more authentic, unless the preacher has a habit of lying to himself. And third, viewing the continuation and culmination of that conversation in the pulpit as an act of self-persuasion shifts the stilted and often mutually resentful relationships between preacher and listener. Things really change when everyone present believes the sermon is meant for everyone present! They begin to feel preached for rather than preached at.

Continuity and Novelty: A Month of Sundays

Whoever invented that folksy phrase "a month of Sundays," it was certainly not a preacher. Commonly used to designate a long period of time, a month of Sundays is for the parish minister, just over half a year of weekly preaching. In fact, for those who take the responsibility seriously, Sundays roll around with such frequency that the discipline of preaching seems almost impossible to sustain. The study time required, not to mention contemplation, meditation, and reflection, gets squeezed out by administrative tasks, staff squabbles, and family errands. Sermons that used to feel like the child of inspiration become the orphan of obligation. They are gotten up and gotten through, more than experienced as *Cor ad Cor Loquitur*—"heart speaks to heart."

For one thing, a gulf exists between those who teach homiletics, and are usually guest preachers in local churches or at preaching conferences and workshops, and parish ministers, who face the same crowd week after week, year after year. For parish ministers, the difficulty of negotiating distance and intimacy is far more pronounced. The guest preacher enjoys all the liberating qualities of novelty. The face is unfamiliar ("Who is this masked man?"), the voice peculiar, and the style is at least an intriguing change, if not a blessed relief from the standard fare. William Sloane Coffin, Jr., knew the benefits of a "tent-making" ministry. He was described once as "blowing in; blowing off; and blowing out."[7]

This is not to say that the intimacy found only in the parish ministry is without benefit. To the contrary, the rapport and trust that are often achieved by pastors cannot be touched by the visiting preacher. The best preaching, day in and day out, is done by local church pastors who know the needs and personalities of their flock. They can weave memory and hope into that "insider" discourse that can only be spoken by family to family. Even so, along with the ease and comfort of such familiarity comes a whole new set of problems with regard to the person in the pulpit.

Human beings tend to fill in lots of personality blanks with mostly positive attributes—especially when it comes to guest preachers. They say: he is traveling because he is famous and therefore much in demand; she agreed to preach to us because we are a friendly and receptive congregation about whom she has heard many good things; he brings the fresh perspective of one not burdened with our internal problems, able to speak the word as clearly and bravely as a midnight rider passing through. Aren't we lucky to hear him? Isn't she lucky to get to preach to us? Don't you wish he were our regular preacher?

Novelty has its benefits: it surrounds the honeymoon, shrouds the stranger in a kindly aura, and cannot be ignored as a factor in the words of Jesus about a prophet being without honor in his own country (Matthew 6). The home folk know your strengths and weaknesses. You are far less likely to be able to sustain a mystical countenance or appear infallibly kind. Before you in the sanctuary sit parishioners with whom you have quarreled in board meetings; to one side of the aisle sits a woman who was released from a short hospital stay three hours before you went to visit her; to the other side, always looking sour and suspicious, is the church's resident member of the John Birch Society, who secretly believes that Jesus was an advance man for the Democratic party. Everything you say sounds like creeping socialism to him.

As their pastor, you may wish that you could fool them, but you can't. They know you. Your voice is nothing special, your favorite Scriptures are not a secret, your annoying habits are well known and predictable, and your politics leak around the edges of statements that you would swear are not political at all. How then is the self-persuading preacher to negotiate the relative benefits of both continuity and novelty?

First of all, continuity is more than a comfort. It is a basic human need. Many a young preacher has crashed and burned in his first parish because he made the deadly mistake of turning the bulletin upside down—changing so many elements of the worship service that the congregation feels a stranger has arrived and razed more than just the parsonage. To make *everything* new is not a sign of bold leadership but insensitivity. When the new cannot be seen as a reinterpretation of what is valid about the old, it looks like chaos, not insight. Part of the reason why some Catholic churches are asking for the Latin Mass again is that for a while everything was guitars and leotards. In other words, novelty must arise out of continuity, not supplant it.

The familiar builds trust and makes deviation and invention tenable to the human psyche. But familiarity also plants the seeds of boredom and creates impediments to communication. Not only can religious language grow tired, but the personality of the preacher can, like an old sweater, become so comfortable and predictable that it neutralizes the possibility that anything very exciting will happen. If the sermon is viewed as an intentional act of self-persuasion, however, the congregation should sense that although the trip will be made by someone they know and trust, the outcome will not be so predictable.

Knowing the soldier makes the outcome of the battle much more important but not necessarily more certain. Understanding that the one who speaks is not exempt from the experience of the words being spoken creates what Kenneth Burke calls "identification," or "consubstantiality," at a whole new level. If Burke is correct when he insists that "if men were not apart from one another, there would be no need for the rhetorician to proclaim their unity."[8] then preaching as self-persuasion might be considered the process through which the separation of human beings from God seeks closure through the preacher's own attempts at reconciliation. Persuasion is a by-product, not a frontal attack. The concept is almost akin to Burke's "pure persuasion," which exists nowhere but is the motivational ingredient in any rhetoric:

Pure persuasion involves the saying of something, not for an extraverbal advantage to be got by the saying, but because of a satisfaction intrinsic to the saying. It summons because it likes the feel of a summons. It would be nonplused if the summons were answered. It attacks because it revels in the sheer syllables of vituperation. . . . It intuitively says, "This is so," purely and simply because this is so.[9]

Here is a view of rhetoric that leaves the impression that the preacher would turn a sermon loose even if no one else were present to hear it. It suggests that communication is proceeding on parallel rather than intersecting lines, much as if the pulpit were turned sideways, and the congregation had to adjust to listening to the preacher talking to the wall. Intimacy is still crucial; after all, "This is my pastor." And yet distance is maintained because the act of submitting to the voice of the text brought forward in a moment of worship is obviously an experience larger than just the preacher's opinion about it, or anything else for that matter.

Continuity makes the trip into the text possible because the listener knows and trusts the traveler, and self-persuasion has rearranged the motives for the trip in a most disarming way. Novelty is guaranteed, however, by virtue of the fact that the tour guide will not be reading a standard script. He will be reacting to the familiar as if to discover it for the first time. Knowing a person intimately is not the same thing as always knowing exactly what that person will say or do. What is renewing about marriage is equally true of homiletics: being so close to someone makes it almost impossible to know who is growing and changing. We don't just feel things *about* them. We feel things *through* them.

On Camera or Holding the Camera?

One of the most dangerous misconceptions about preaching is that *personal* means autobiographical. The metaphor of self-persuasion is not to be mistaken for an excuse to turn the pulpit into a confessional, to fill the air with personal reminiscences, to put one's hand upon one's own pulse and call it theology. Hans Van Der Geest writes:

No one in a worship service expects the preacher's own experience to be the source of the gospel. Just as in dialectical theology, humility threatens to turn into its opposite. If preachers want to be so modest that they only speak about their own experiences, then the worship services are turned into assemblies where many people are supposed to be interested in the experiences of a single individual. [10]

Although it is true to a certain extent that all preaching is self-disclosure, what is meant by this is that in preaching one *says* more than is *said*, or less, since every piece of literature (performed or not) is inescapably biographical. What it does not mean is that the person of the preacher is directly or indirectly the subject of every sermon.

Again we seem to be dealing with paradox, but such is the case whenever profound truth is at stake: its opposite lies close by to warn us against the loss of dialectic, haunting us to avoid simple-mindedness with its refrain—"but on the other hand." A preacher may put a tremendous amount of herself into a sermon without the sermon being about herself, nor about what she thinks of this, that, or the other. It just so happens that every sermon is the product of a human being overhearing Scripture from a particular vantage point, in a moment of time in the vernacular of a particular culture, who is then moved to recreate her experience with the text in ways that are highly idiosyncratic.

How else could it be? Those sermons marked "Good for Any Occasion" are really good for none. No stronger argument can be made against stealing and preaching the sermons of others than that such rhetorical plagiarism simply doesn't work. The voice, the eyes, the inflections all betray the lie—this is someone else talking. An observant and honest spouse can always tell: "I liked your sermon today . . . especially the part when *you* were talking." R. E. C. Browne reminds us that rhetoric arising from the sentences and paragraphs of others will short-circuit the extemporaneous and authentic quality of speech because "the rhythm of [his] thinking gets into the rhythm of his speaking." Quoting a favorite poet, Browne continues: "You don't devise a rhythm, the rhythm is the person, and the sentence but a radiograph of personality."[11]

A hollow sound coming from the pulpit reveals many things: that the conversation with the text never happened or was superficial; that nothing touched a nerve, caused a stir, or raised a genuine question; that no passion was originated and therefore none can be disseminated. After all, what isn't incarnate cannot be made manifest. What hasn't been put away cannot be retrieved. The preacher who has discovered no way to pour himself into a text will find it impossible to become a channel through which a sermon is poured out. It is precisely at the level of such deficiencies that the temptation to substitute personality for passion arise. And yet the fact is, personality can authenticate passion, but it can never create it.

Consider again the unique profession that is ministry. Ordinary men and women are supposed to pass the precepts and dispositions of the Gospel through the framework of their everyday lives. Preaching demands that these lives be lived in a largely interpretive posture, searching for the lessons of life and the words to express them. The listener has a right to expect that wisdom will shape personality but will resent the impression that personality has shaped wisdom. Self-persuading preachers get in the way, so to speak, in order to get out of the way.

In the famous definition of preaching by Phillips Brooks, "truth mediated through personality," the emphasis must be upon the word *mediated*. Personality channels truth, and in so doing may either enhance it or distract from it. But the *source* of the urgency that makes preaching contagious is to be found in the shared respect for the text as a formidable conversation partner, not in the personality of the preacher as a formidable conversant. Preaching as self-persuasion is both because of and in spite of personality, as Browne says best: "To hear a minister of the Word preach often should not be to know him better but to know yourself better and only to increase your knowledge of him through what you realize he has shown you about yourself."[12]

One of the simplest and most helpful descriptions of this tension was overheard at a meeting of the Academy of Homiletics. The preacher "holds the camera," but is not necessarily "on camera." We stand with the preacher as she describes the walk from text to sermon, but we do not keep seeing the preacher everywhere she goes. We see what she sees, and feel what she feels, and are rewarded by how keenly she watches the world and passes its light through the prism of Christian faith.

Many talented users of the language never preach with the power they might otherwise attain for the simple reason that they do not listen long enough, or look hard enough, or feel deeply enough *before* they start speaking. Somewhere between the whisper of the study and the shout of the sermon, a real human being stands responsible for the amplification that only passion can provide. Because the sermon's principle purpose is to evoke rather than to edify, the self-persuading preacher can no more leave self out of the process than a congregation can accept conclusions reached on their behalf by someone else. The very term *self*-persuasion means that *selves* are doing the persuading. No one else can do it for us.

By the same token, one self does not persuade another self directly, and this is critically important to remember when it comes to what is called "the cult of personality." To hold the camera and to pan the scenes of this world on behalf of the examined life is necessarily personal, but these are rhetorical home movies, not Hollywood productions. It's not *who* is in the scene that matters. It is *how* the scene matters to the who that's in it. Listeners aren't just interested in where the preacher has been; they want to be taken along; they want to draw their own conclusions. They want admirable company on the journey, not an expert in the meaning of the journey.

All of this is to say that personality counts enormously but not ultimately. It is more important that the person of the preacher not contradict the message than that it should be expected to compensate for it. What the congregation needs from the preacher is the same thing the preacher needs from himself: honesty. To invite a congregation to overhear you talking about important things in real, honest, and relevant ways is to give them permission, by example, to do the same. We listen to talk meaningfully, and then we talk meaningfully enough to be worth listening to. It is a humanizing and contagious process.

It is also more than a philosophical and theoretical concept. It has real, concrete, practical implications for writing and delivering sermons. The time has come to get specific.

Chapter 7
The Self-Persuading Preacher and Language

You can never be a poet unless you are fascinated by words—their sounds and shapes and meanings—and have them whirling about in your head all the time.

—C. Day Lewis

The Nonnegotiable: A Love of Words

Preaching as self-persuasion requires a keen and compulsive respect for language. Words are not just a bag of tools for reporting on the world, they are little pieces of the world, puffs of air that only seem weightless. Leaving no track as they arc over silence, they make their mark on the soul: teasing or troubling, building up or tearing down, confirming the angels or etching further an already wounded world.

Because the self-persuading preacher must talk to himself in meaningful ways, so that his listeners will talk to themselves in meaningful ways, the business of choosing and speaking words is more than just a hobby—it is a quest. Whereas the traditional focus of preaching has been edification, this paradigm places *evocation* at the heart of the sermon experience. Edification comes after examining the meaning of what has been evoked, for what has not been stored in the heart is soon erased by time. David Buttrick writes:

> We live in language. Words are not merely stuff to thicken bulky dictionaries. No, words whirl about us; they give life significance and indeed make life possible. We are "Homo loquens." We "do" within language. Could we build a house, conduct business, or run governments without words? No won-

der that, in the ancient myth of Babel, tower builders gave up building when their common language broke down. Without words, legislative chambers would be silent, airports stopped, courtrooms emptied, schoolrooms closed, and households reduced to a gesturing of strangers.[1]

To use language that sparks a new conversation in the listener, the self-persuading preacher must approach the selection, assembly, and delivery of words as the poets do. Words must be weighed and measured not for their utility, but for their effect and theological precision. Then they should be uttered as a reflection of the same feelings they seek to evoke.

Ironically, some of the most articulate preachers ignore the Bible as a source of instruction in the use of language. They translate the rich and earthy metaphors of Scripture into propositions or exhortations, requiring little more from the listener than agreement or disagreement. Yet to be a truly "biblical" preacher, one must pay close attention to the source and try to understand why the Gospel is an extended story and contains an encyclopedia of indirect literary forms.

To preach a parable "parabolically," or present a dialogue dialogically, or slip the language of mythology past the guarded ears of rationality, the self-persuading preacher must be concerned not just with what words say, but with what words do. Often those who know better than to take Scripture literally, and who argue that revelation is not found in propositional form, turn around and seek to communicate the Gospel in unequivocally propositional form. In this way, ministers of the word are schizophrenic when it comes to their theology of language. Fearing a loss of control, they tend to offer "what can only be apprehended by faith as if it were capable of being grasped by reason alone."[2]

The surest mark of a self-persuading preacher is that she takes delight in words for their own sake. She loves what they can do when they are turned loose in a sanctuary full of friends. She demonstrates an almost childish affection for words as emotional music, as notes in the score of the symphony of human ideas. Words don't just tunnel us toward the light; they create light. They are characters of sound, dressed in breath, pitch, and volume, trooping their way through the air and into our hearts.

They are the most important visitors of the morning, and if the preacher receives them, the congregation will receive them. For it is in taking delight in words that we teach listeners to take delight in words. It is in loving the sound and sense of an utterance that we train listeners to expect, even to crave, authentic communication. "For by your words you will be justified, and by your words you will be condemned" (Matt. 12:37).

For some strange reason, even in this day when the pulpit remains for many a cartoon of irrelevancy, ministers still cling to the fiction that their words need only be truthful, not compelling. Language at its highest level is for poets and playwrights, they say, and not for the somber business of the kingdom. Preaching must be more than entertainment, and so for millions, it is not *even* entertaining. A teacher of preaching writes:

> Words can be strung together into sentences and piled into paragraphs, words that are religious, biblical, and true, and yet do nothing. They do not raise a window, open a door, build a fire, or offer a chair. They are said, they collect below the pulpit, and are swept out on Monday morning. . . . So what does this audience want, oratory? No; they want some insight.[3]

Such insight can only be achieved if the preacher steps into the pulpit ready to talk about what he has heard in ways that create a new hearing. To do this he has shopped for words, hunted for the plumpest and ripest words, thumping them against his ear and listening for the sound of quality. What is soft or bruised is put back; he digs down and finds something fresher, or he moves on. If this sounds like compulsive behavior, it is exactly that. But consider the alternative. All words are not created equal, nor are all sentences. Some verbs are strong and clear, doing what they say, whereas others slink about, falling out of the corners of the mouth and getting lost in the carpet. Some adjectives call to the senses without overpowering them, while others only obscure what they are trying to draw attention to.

Most sermons take twice as long to get started as they should. Running off and leaving people is not advisable, but think how much more invigorating it is to jump the moving cable car, than to be waved into the standing taxi. A student in a public speaking class recently demonstrated the power of the quick start. She was giving a speech of self-introduction, and instead of the usual rambling description of the location of her home town, its population, and major exports, she said: "I come from a town that none of you have ever visited, but all of you have been to. It has a Dairy Queen, a set of railroad tracks, and a Wal-Mart. I hung out at the Dairy Queen, thought about death when I crossed the railroad tracks, and dreamed about a dress that can't be bought at Wal-Mart."[4] With this brief paragraph, the student gathered up everyone in the room without a single innocuous phrase like, "I'm here today to tell you just how much we have in common in this world in which we live."

Preaching must recognize the difference between the eye and the ear, and its language must be both rich and sparse. Preachers should employ what English teachers call the "active voice," and the present tense more than the past. Short sentences, the vernacular of the day, and an honesty about what communicates should infuse the self-persuading sermon. A healthy way to measure all this is to not let public discourse deviate too far from private discourse. We talk to ourselves more like Hemingway than like Wordsworth. The eye can linger, back-track, and tarry where it will. But the ear wants to get down to business.

Most of all, the self-persuading preacher should talk to others the way she likes being talked to. She should be the first to edit the tired cliché, pare down the rambling story, and choose words that create a rhetorical experience with unity of purpose and fluidity of movement. After all, she doesn't want to bore herself. And self-persuasion is consequential: the more disciplined and creative, the more passionate and contagious.

More Description, Less Explanation

A self-persuading sermon succeeds not because the preacher is able to hand over increments of edification, but because images and ideas are offered up that when reflected upon prove edifying. The object is not to make a delivery but to manage an encounter. If the experience of the text is to be made contagious, the preacher must avoid simply explaining it and recommending it.

He will seek to reflect the meaning of the text, not simply reflect upon it. Using the power of descriptive rather than conceptual language, the sermon is to achieve what Martin Heidegger calls the primary function of language: letting be what is through evocative images rather than conceptual structures.[5]

Because persuasion is located in the response of the listener, careful attention must be paid to what kind of language produces what kind of response, and how the associative functions of the mind work. If biblical concepts are severed from biblical characters—devoid of taste, touch, sight, smell, and sound—the listener may be stirred to sleepy agreement or polite deference but there will hardly be persuasion. Persuasion takes passion, and passion is generated in the presence of something real.

For the listener, this means that the authentic is validated by the comparable. To recognize a universal human experience is to be awakened and aroused: breath lost through fear, candles snuffed out by a sudden wind, the steaming bloody miracle of birth, the dull ache of loneliness, the delirium of love, the fever of jealousy. When Thomas Wolf describes the tedium of life as the "dusty racket of our days," he does not offer an explanation of boredom, nor does he elaborate on the existential dimensions of meaninglessness. He just turns a beautiful phrase, and we fill in the blanks.

The mind is a gallery hung with images, not a giant filing cabinet full of carefully reasoned concepts. When the preacher leads a tour of these universal images, she does it by sharing her own, not by explaining everyone else's. It can be argued that attitudes and values are more intimately connected with these images than with any detached concept relating to them. Poets and novelists know that changing an attitude has more to do with replacing an image than with shuffling a new idea through the trap doors of the intellect:

> Images are replaced not by concepts but by other images, and that quite slowly. Long after a man's head has consented to the preacher's idea, the old images still hang in the heart. But not until that image is replaced is he really a changed man . . . this takes time, because the longest trip a person takes is that from head to heart.[6]

When the object is self-persuasion, impression precedes expression. And what has been experienced is not translated into the semantics of an argument. The image *is* the argument, and the sermon is a form of imaging. Contrary to conventional wisdom about the sermon illustrations being incidental, a pleasant diversion, or comic relief, the self-persuading preacher cannot regard descriptive material as an accessory to the real sermon. Much that the Gospel commends is not rational anyway, and when speaking of grace, forgiveness, and agape love, the minister would be wise to point to and describe what he cannot explain: "To speak the truth is to be more than a purveyor of pious information: it is to show the way to think and not to offer the results of thought; it is to sharpen a man's perception rather than tell him what to see; it is to describe to him the love of God but not to define it."[7]

The reader may object here by reminding us that the sermon should constitute an argument, that it should advocate the Gospel. But we are only saying that the most effective argument is not an argument at all, rather it is a series of images that flow from an amplified conversation—strung together by a germinal idea that acts like the string of a necklace. Browne alludes to this when he says, "The effective speaker is always more concerned with making the appropriate allusions than with trying to ensure that the steps of his argument will move logically toward their proper conclusion."[8]

If this is beginning to sound formless, chaotic, or too much like the stream-of-consciousness school of composition, then we must remember this: Nothing about poetic language releases the preacher from an obligation to careful construction and ordered movement in the sermon. Nor can it take the place of all direct, propositional discourse. A listener is never to get the impression that a metaphor is marvelous but hasn't the slightest relevance to the subject at hand. As language gets more abstract, the need for rhetorical discipline does not diminish, it increases. We are not reciting personal poetry journals in public. We are preaching on the great themes of love and hate, sin and redemption, life and death.

But we are not being asked to issue a brief on these topics.

Rather, we are called to lift them up and let them speak for themselves. Ideas and emotions are not merely discussed, rather they are *exposed* through descriptive language. Those who stand at the edge of the Grand Canyon and babble on about its depth, estimated age, and mineral composition are in danger of being shoved over the edge. Who cares if this is the "showcase of the forces of erosion?" What teaches us is the Silence.

Preachers are too eager to make sure that everyone understands, that everyone gets it. This inevitably means that too much of the obvious is explained, and too little of the mysterious is described. We are not using symbolic language to achieve some sort of conceptual precision, rather we are using metaphors to generate the insight that comes from recognizing common human experience. Dr. Austin Farr writes to counter the findings of those in the general semantics movement who believed that words could be used like slide rules: "There is a current and exceedingly stupid doctrine that symbol evokes emotion, and exact prose states reality. Nothing could be further from the truth: exact prose abstracts from reality, symbol presents it. And for that reason, symbols have some of the many-sidedness of wild nature."[9]

"Many-sidedness" is an appropriate image, for description is akin to the turning of a gem in just the right light. At any moment, a facet may catch the sun and light up an unsuspecting face. It depends on where you happen to be sitting—not upon how many carats, how much weight, or what may be happening on the back side. The preacher with a keen eye and vivid powers of description makes keen watchers of the congregation and swells their self-persuasive vocabulary as well.

For example, fear will not be explained but described as a taste in the corner of the mouth, a tightness in the chest, and fingers that drum the table. Envy is not just one of the seven deadly sins, it is the muttering, acid face of a childless woman who finds fault with all good fortune, and shines her bitter light on the dark side of every happiness. Regret is more than an entry in the dictionary ("to feel sorrow or remorse"). It is a middle-aged man, walking bone tired to a job he hates, wondering why the little boy he never tucked in won't talk to him about being a teenager. He worked overtime; now he's out of time.

Images in the sermon should be concrete and particular, because we do not respond to motherhood in general, but to the plight of a mother in particular. But they must also be limited and incomplete, otherwise the listener is left without work to do. In fact, the most dangerous thing about becoming poetic is that we sometimes become overbearing. If our images and metaphors can get in the way in order to get out of the way, then we will have achieved real communication. But if they live for themselves, begging notice and admiration, then they fail to spark the conversations we desire. This tension, between what is offered and what is withheld, is so crucial to self-persuasion that it deserves further comment.

The Aesthetics of Restraint

One of the more unfortunate but accurate caricatures of the preacher is of someone who doesn't know when to quit. In the evangelical zeal to persuade, more is always better, and letting up is to be equated with resignation. If three examples are good, why not six? If all that matters is getting a listener to yield, then why not assume the role of debater, arguing not only for your position but against all others? If the inside of the church represents your point of view, and the outside all others, why not run around locking all the windows and closing all the doors and then stand up to say, "Good choice!" Because self-persuasion requires more than getting the listener to say "uncle."

The perception of choice is what differentiates persuasion from coercion. Self-persuasion assumes an almost reckless trust in the power of the truth to prevail so long as ideas are made irresistible but not mandatory. Because truth is appropriated, not transferred, the language of the sermon will function, as Heidegger maintained, as Being itself coming to us in a "clearing-concealing" role.[10] We accept the fact that all language is imprecise, that all idioms are ambiguous, and that finally, what we talk about is transcendent and cannot be captured in finite terms. When the subject matter is huge, the words need not always be: "In a sense the sermon does not matter, what matters is what the preacher cannot say because the ineffable remains the ineffable and all that can be done is to make gestures toward it with the finest words that can be used."[11]

Our efforts in the pulpit must be more like courtroom sketches than photographs. Leaving the listener with lines to draw and profiles to be sketched into whole faces is more than desirable— it is the objective. Given everything, the listener is literally left with nothing. In rhetoric, to be too thorough is also to deprive. This means that a pair of vital restraints are required in every sermon. The first has to do with the thesis, or germinal idea. The second has to do with the construction and expression of ideas that support the thesis.

Since a sermon about everything is a sermon about nothing, the preacher must first establish a controlling or germinal idea. Without a thesis, all plausible ideas orbit equidistant from a nonexistent center. Nothing can bid for space on the page because the page is not defined: no heading, no margins. Ideas troop across the stage of the mind auditioning for a part in the sermon, but the preacher has no plot, and without a plot, can't begin to pick characters, much less arrange them into scenes. What is true of creating sermons is true of composing music, and Igor Stravinsky has reminded us that "whatever diminishes constraint diminishes strength."[12]

No preacher has the right to work on points until he has gotten the point. Equally distracting is the tendency some preachers have to overdescribe. There is good reason why we pick one flower at a time to smell: too many can shut down the senses. Likewise with the preacher who is intent upon painting a verbal picture so intense and detailed that no one will miss it. He forgets the function of backgrounds, complementary colors, and blank spaces, which serve silently to push forward what is to register and be enlarged upon. Too many details smack of unreality, not reality: "Let the minister pile upon his people long sentences about the 'inspiring and moving' and he thereby drains the occasion of all possibility to inspire or to move. . . . It is a child's art that places both eyes on one side of the head to assure observers of the profile that the person portrayed had two eyes."[13]

Economy of language, especially descriptive language, is always in service to, and out of respect for, the listener's capacity to contribute. Adjectives are used sparingly because they announce ahead of time the very attributes that the listener needs to perceive and announce as his own. But more important still, a lean language style is inviting because it alludes to the existence of much that is hidden, the proverbial tip of the iceberg—much that is hidden gives meaning to the little that is said. Those with much to say do not have to be talking all the time. Instead, they will, as Ezra Pound suggests, "crowd maximum meaning into the single phrase, pregnant, charged, and luminous from within."[14] Speakers, like lovers, must be coy, otherwise there is no anticipation. The most intimate emotions, directly disgorged, usually push us away.

Such restraint is difficult for ministers because they believe that the stakes of the battle require that no weapon be left untried. The illusion is grounded in a quantitative notion of authority:

> What ministers of the word say may seem too little to live on, but they must not go beyond their authority in a mistaken attempt to make their authority strong and clear. That going beyond is always the outcome of an aesthetic anxiety, or a sign that the man of God has succumbed to the temptation to speak as a god, to come in his own name and to be his own authority.[15]

The same preacher who issues this warning recognizes that in the mad rush to make God obvious, we can obscure God. Sermons, he says, should contain an "essential untidiness" where things are never too clear, lest they appear false.

Again, this fits the paradigm of self-persuasion because the sermon is a trip not a destination, and the listener is supposed to have the last word. If the preacher talks all the time, building a room of words and then furnishing it as well, the listeners have what builders call a turn-key house. The buyer walks in, plops down in an easy chair, and never breaks a sweat. But think how foreign such a room would seem! There is something about that first night—with boxes as a dinner table, take-out Chinese food, and blank walls—that promises a transformation only the owner can provide. If it is true that grace can fill only empty space, then what preachers must avoid is the bloated sermon. The preacher may mean well, but when a "speaker works overtime, the listener is left unemployed."[16]

Again, the tool to measure such restraint is the preacher's own ear. Listening closely to the way we talk to ourselves teaches us much about the proper way of talking to others. All that can be assumed is left unsaid, and what is formed into speech is sparse, nonpropositional, and usually in service to an emotion that remains in the realm of silence. Questions are the mainstay of intrapersonal communication, but the heart is very often left to provide the answer: "What *did* she mean by that comment anyway?" Sometime we mutter to ourselves in ways that seem exclamatory on the surface but whose real intent is probative: "I don't think I can take this anymore."

The level of intimacy between a preacher and a congregation makes it possible to say less and less as times goes by and to accomplish the communication of more and more. Like partners in a long and fruitful marriage, the language becomes coded and sparse, but the nod is there, the wink, the knowing smile. Silence is not frightening but rather a fertile bed on which words lie, the respite that invites the listener to fill the void or let it be. No self-persuading preacher need interrupt herself to fill the air with such nonsensical phrases as "We see" or "We find" or "In this world today in which we live." That's not the way we talk to ourselves. Neither should it be the way we talk to others.

In preaching, what is left unsaid may be as important as what is said. Especially when one is working under the conviction that people must, in the end, persuade themselves of the truth, it becomes vitally important that the listener understand that not everything that *can* be said, *will* be said. The ultimate goal of the self-persuading sermon is to converse with and about God in such a way that the listener wants in on the line—to make those who overhear this irresistible conversation feel compelled to say, "Excuse me, I couldn't help but hear you . . . I know just what you mean . . . once the very same thing happened to me . . . very much as you describe it."

The Structure of Anticipation

If the listener is to become a truly active partner in the persuasion process, not only must the preacher use language like a poet, and exercise restraint like an artist, but he must also build into the structure of the sermon a sense of *anticipation*. Preaching that engages listeners is by nature a dramatic act. Although many clergy are uncomfortable with the idea of the sermon as drama, it is inescapable if the object is self-persuasion. In the theater, listeners are seldom directly addressed; they respond to what they overhear and are drawn into scenes that unfold as actors negotiate conflict and resolution oblivious to the audience. They do not stop to explain or interpret the meaning of their lines. They act. The audience enters the drama vicariously.

The extent to which the listeners experience the drama depends on two things: plot and identification. Kenneth Burke has written that all communication is essentially dramatic, and the resolution of conflict is contagious by virtue of identification. "Eloquence is simply the end of art, and thus its essence,"[17] he writes. Further, literature is designed to "do something" for the writer, the reader, or the listener—to elicit a response of some kind, where words are thought of as "acts upon a scene," and a symbolic act is the "dancing of an attitude."[18]

What a marvelous definition of preaching: the dancing of an attitude. Separated from God and from each other, Burke calls this division, and the need to overcome it, the principle "motive" for rhetoric. Watching and listening as the preacher struggles to close the gap, the listener struggles as well, creating what Burke calls "cosubstantiality." He could have been writing about self-persuasion when he said:

> Identification can also be an "end," as "when people earnestly yearn to identify themselves with some group or other." They are thus not necessarily acted upon by a conscious external agent, but may act upon themselves to this end. Identification "includes the realm of transcendence."[19]

A full analysis of preaching in Burkean terms is not possible here, but the notion of identification is central to the idea that the sermon is an experience of shared human drama. Preachers who attempt to negotiate the distance between the ideal world of the Kingdom and the real world of human sin are engaged in dramatic acts motivated by what Burke would call "guilt." His unconventional use of this word is altogether appropriate because it is out of this perceived failure to achieve the perfection God intended that ministers are compelled to attempt reconciliation between persons and between the community of faith and its Gospel credo.

It cannot be said too often: the self-persuading preacher is not reporting on an encounter with Scripture. The sermon *is* an encounter with Scripture. Approached by means of what scholars are calling the "second naiveté," the preacher anticipates that the Bible still has much to say, even to this age (or especially to this age). He will not "write out" that anticipation in the structure of the sermon, as if the hunt is his responsibility and only the spoils belong to the congregation. The sermon will recreate the struggle that gave birth to insight and preserve the plot that emerged as a new hearing took shape in this journey we call interpretation.

Too often, preachers assume that their job is to get a head start in the study, so that listeners can be spared the exegetical legwork, the first irreverent questions, or the doubts that accompany any honest reading of an ancient text. But the truth is, the preacher's first response is not unlike that of the listener: What *has* this got to do with anything? Who cares? Is there a word from God in this peculiar and primitive scrap? It is tragic that so many who sit before the pulpit believe they are the *only* ones who ask such questions. The preacher must understand instantly, they assume—otherwise how else could she rise to explain it all with such an effortless smile, awash in a saccharin certainty?

Self-persuasion generates passion precisely because there is nothing as authentic, or as contagious, as a speaker who is retracing the journey of insight and reexperiencing it all at the same time. The art of structuring anticipation into a sermon is not just a strategy for the listener, it is an indulgence for the preacher. It is an art practiced with a certain degree of selfishness, as when joke-tellers revel in the concealing of a punch line they already know, or storytellers let the plot encircle them even though they know how the story ends.

What matters ultimately in rhetoric, as in all literary experiences, is *movement*. Sermon form is important only as it serves movement. The self-persuading preacher has to have some idea what the destination is, in order to structure the journey. The route by which the listener travels will be determined by the nature of the message to be communicated. But two things will not change: movement that creates curiosity, appetite, suspense, involvement, and so on; and a message that provides the means of satisfying what has been aroused.

Strange as it may sound, a minister who hasn't written a sermon she wishes to listen to is a minister not worth hearing. The preacher knows what will be said but uses the sermon to know it better, to feel it more deeply, to experience it "publicly." The unspoken principle is, "Wait until they hear what I heard." And the eagerness to speak is in part a result of their own anticipation: "Wait until I hear again what I heard." The sermon becomes a builder of faith, as well as an act of faith. Preaching as self-persuasion is akin to Edmund Steimle's assertion that the posture of every sermon is determined by the prayer, "Lord I believe; help my unbelief."

This can be accomplished if sermons will only mimic the nature of acquired insight, not subvert it. Most of what we learn comes inductively, and seldom by three points and a joke. For example, we do not rise from our beds in the morning, blink our eyes, and state the thesis for the day: "Compassion must be organized!" Instead we stumble around to fill the coffee cup and notice out the window a Salvation Army truck. The teenage driver seems uninterested, lost in his headphones. We recall being pestered about having our discardables on the curb by Tuesday. The truck is loud, rusty, and running on bald tires and borrowed time.

Then suddenly it occurs to us: without this structure, without this routine, without this route, things would not be given or collected in sufficient quantity. We take another sip of coffee and ponder how much that is good is *compelled* through order and resolve, and how little that is good is done on the strength of warm, fuzzy thoughts alone. That's when we conclude: compassion must be organized.

If the listeners are to be given a chance at reaching this conclusion, then they will have to be invited to join in the waking up as well. Standard rhetorical form may not always work, but neither can it be ignored. That is, although not every sermon will have a formal introduction, it matters very much how every sermon begins. Although it may not have a formal body, it will matter very much what comes in between. And although it may not have a conclusion that summarizes main points, provides closure, or refers back to the introduction, it matters very much how every sermon ends. Likewise with transitions, one of the most difficult and important of the rhetorical arts. They may not all be perfect, like Janus, looking backward and forward, reviewing and previewing. But they will still need to be there, smoothing the turns in the road, or the listener will find the going rough.

The sermon may begin in what appears to be the middle, or even the end of the experience of the text. It may intentionally confuse by commencing in dialogue without context or identifiable participants. It may use flashback, gradually framed and focused by remembrances. It may strip away all the conventions of an introduction by speaking a single word, confessing the confusion that surrounds it for the preacher, and then proceeding to structure the sermon as spokes radiating out from this etymological hub.

The number of possible sermon structures is unlimited, and most preaching suffers not from inventiveness but from the lack of it. Only one constant needs to apply to each and every structure: the systematic creation of appetite through anticipation, and a creative means for satisfaction. Not every sermon needs to move in the same manner, but every sermon must move. Sermons that demand participation without creating appetite are like catered meals: carried in and dropped on the table full-born, without the kitchen ritual and the encouragement of the nose, the appetite is taken by surprise, even suppressed. Anticipation may be life's chief pleasure. In preaching, it is the first obligation of form.

The Primal Power of Story

Everything we have discussed so far (poetics, restraint, and the structure of anticipation) relates to the form of the sermon. That form should always be considered subordinate to, and even consumed in, the service of that *movement* that makes the sermon an organism—an integrated, engaging event in the world of sound. The Bible itself contains an impressive catalogue of forms, and a closer look at how parables, aphorisms, hymns, creeds, baptismal formulas, prayers, farewell speeches, and doxologies function to communicate in an oral tradition is immensely helpful to the self-persuading preacher.

The oral/aural nature of preaching can hardly be overstated, and the Scriptures bear constant testimony to the fact that before any written documents were gathered together, the community of faith lived by speaking and hearing words. This means that no matter what form the preacher chooses, two considerations remain paramount: does the form of the sermon reflect the content of the Scripture and what it intends to communicate, and is the writing done on behalf of the sermon event shaped by the *ear* of the listener rather than by the *eye* of the author?

The object is not simply to get the sermon written but to get it heard. This means that whether an outline is preferred, or a manuscript, the notes used for preaching will prompt and guide an oral event. There is constant discussion among preachers as to what form sermon notes should take, or even whether notes should be used at all. But one thing is agreed upon: the notes are not to be confused with the sermon. To "read" a sermon is truly a contradiction in terms. As the eye tracks across the page, sending cognitive information to the brain about *what* to say, the voice and body have no way of simultaneously preparing a *means* of expression. After all, deciding which words to speak and how to speak them at the same time is no small feat. Sense must come ahead of syntax, or the dreaded monotone sets in.

Inflection, vocal variety, emphasis, and energy are all born of familiarity, confidence, and an unself-conscious desire to hear words that sound like what they mean. Likewise, those words in concert form sentences that mean, and the sentences conspire together to form paragraphs that mean. Meaning tumbles over itself, and in a sense, the self-persuading preacher sings.

All words are not created equal: ask the ear. Flat lines in rhetoric mean exactly what they mean in the hospital. But words that rise and fall from the mouth of someone who understands that meaning is a function of "vocal choreography" create the very semantic waves which make communication a dramatic act.

There are many rhetorical devices for enriching the experience of the sermon: the well-posed question; the use of irony, humor, exaggeration, and suspense. Lively and expressive dialogue, especially when the identity of the speakers is made obvious by vocal inflection and not encumbered with "he said . . . and then she said." But by far the most effective, the most dependable, and the most endearing of all rhetorical forms for self-persuasion is the extended narrative. Nothing enriches the experience of listening to a sermon like the well-placed, well-told story.

The power of narrative to entice and involve the listener is without equal. Its durability as a channel for sacred truth is testified to by every culture whose history and defining values are wrapped in myth and passed from generation to generation as a collection of stories. Those who insist that narrative is too flimsy, too fictional, too childlike and bedtime-ish to carry the heavy freight of theology must find a way to refute one simple fact: the Gospel is mostly a collection of stories, woven together to give us the Story. In a sense, the extended narrative is the consummate example of a literary device that consumes itself in service to the experience it seeks to create. Stories are by nature not out to announce their intentions, to prove a point, or to insist that some rational, propositional conclusion be drawn from the experience of listening. They ask for nothing except to be heard, and once they begin the listener's posture changes. Stories free the listener to enter into the experience at any level, or not at all— granting what they often embody: anonymity. They are usually about someone else, somewhere else, doing something else that does not demand immediate interpretation. They do not come dressed as teachers but as entertainers.

In self-persuasion, stories are indispensable because they place the listener in the posture of overhearing. This is the posture of the preacher with regard to the text, and both the listener and the preacher with regard to the sermon. Because stories are a detached and indirect form of communication, they can be enjoyed for their own sake, suspended for a blessed moment from the clash of opinions and the tendency of listeners to judge discourse primarily on its source rather than on its content. Stories have a way of getting free of the preacher, to everyone's delight. There are few veterans of the pulpit who have not noticed the palpable shift that occurs in a sanctuary when a gripping story, well told, begins to work its magic. Listening shifts so distinctly into a higher gear that an energy is released, the faces (and sometimes the bodies) draw forward and expressions become unguarded and animated. It is no wonder that Jesus taught mostly in parables.

Narrative works because it is governed by the same essential tension of distance and intimacy that regulate what goes on between the preacher and the text and the preacher and the congregation. Stories invite participation precisely because they do not demand it. We recognize in stories our own story, not because someone pried into our secrets, but because the story safely bears them in its characters—allowing us to recognize ourselves, understand ourselves, even teach ourselves. Furthermore, stories have a shape that gives them the first ingredient of a good sermon: movement. They are compressed events relating action, dialogue, and emotion. They do not just try to *say* something true; they *do* something that is recognized as true.

In short, narrative works because it is the very form of life itself. "We dream in narrative, daydream in narrative, remember, anticipate, hope, despair, believe, doubt, plan, revise, criticize, construct, gossip, learn, hate, and love by narrative."[20] Stories are the most potent stimuli for self-persuasion because they unfold on their own, without anxious regard for the listener. We are drawn to stories precisely because they do not need us. They do not scold, press their point, quiz, repeat themselves, or insist on being understood. It is no wonder that when a preacher tells a story, he can hear himself most clearly. He is not just breathing life into every word; the words are breathing life into him: "A narrative is told with distance and sustains it in that the story unfolds on its own, seemingly only casually aware of the hearer, and yet all the while the narrative is inviting and beckoning the listener to participation in its anticipation, struggle, and resolution."[21]

It is wise to remember that narrative form does not always mean *story* in the classic sense. Sermons can have a narrative quality without possessing distinct story units. Many other rhetorical forms create a feeling of narrative without requiring a standard story line. Any speech that "ties itself to the life of a larger community . . . has memory and hope . . . touching all the keys on the board rather than only intellectual, or emotional or volitional" is narrativelike.[22]

The most important effect of narrative, however, is upon the narrator. She reexperiences the story while telling it. Her delight, her confusion, her surprise, her anger is a signal to the listener—this is worth hearing. Again, the best joke tellers *prepare* you to laugh, give you many opportunities for little laughs before the big laugh, and prime your humor in advance. By the time they reach the punch line, it feels like your punch line. When the self-persuading preacher is finished, you feel like the insight is a collective endeavor.

No one should make the case that all a sermon needs to be great is a couple of good stories. Narrative alone cannot communicate sufficiently to exclude other rhetorical forms. But whoever throws away narrative, claiming not to be a "story preacher," throws away the heaviest piece of artillery in the arsenal of self-persuasion. For the nonstory preacher, not only will ideas seldom leave the runway of rational discourse and fly into the wide open spaces where the imagination and the spirit conspire to teach, but the preacher will miss perhaps the best opportunity to *demonstrate* self persuasion.

Many a professor of homiletics has noticed what happens when the student begins to tell a story. Unmistakable changes take place. The eyes come up off the page, since the story is likely to be more internalized than other material. The face changes, and as the tale unfolds, the voice reflects more accurately and unself-consciously the meaning of the words. The whole person seems infused with a more authentic energy. What is happening? The preacher is listening.

Some truths exist apart from, even in spite of, our best efforts to communicate them. In stories, the preacher can step back and see that wisdom has its own light, its own future, makes its own way. It is at such moments that preaching can becomes almost translucent—full of the spirit. Words come out of the preacher's mouth and curl back with grace upon his own ear. He says things he hadn't planned to say because he is feeling things he hadn't planned to feel. Entangled in his own sermon, he becomes wise to his own words.

The Preacher's Ear as Editor-in-Chief

It has been mentioned in passing that a principle cause of bad preaching is deafness. This was not a misprint. Nor is the charge being leveled at the listener. Rather, it is often the case that the preacher has quit listening. She still *hears*—the mispronounced word, the twisted phrase, the grammatical error. But she no longer *listens* experientially nor is her speech in any significant way self-monitored. This may be the most difficult concept in self-persuasion to explain, but speaking and listening at the same time is truly an art.

The object is to be consistent in the process of overhearing. Just as the text is overheard, so must the sermon be overheard. And although this sounds like a form of homiletic narcissism, there is a difference between preaching to oneself and listening in on what one is preaching. The former would be indulgent, if not pathetic. The latter is the secret to rhetoric that does what it says. Furthermore, by speaking and listening simultaneously, the preacher models the very listening behavior that he intends for those in the pew. His self-consciousness about language—his playful, enigmatic, unpredictable response to an idea at work on all ears in the house—sets a self-persuasive tone in the sanctuary. It looks and sounds like fun, like something matters, like the sermon is a dangerous, marvelous thing.

One way to understand the role of the preacher's ear in self-persuasion is as a kind of editor-in-chief. Every day, in the execu-

tive offices of big city newspapers, a meeting takes place to decide what goes on page one. It is a bidding war of sorts, because
there is usually considerable disagreement about what constitutes
"real news." Not everything can go on page one, even though
every story seems deserving to its author. But somebody has to
decide, and the decision is based on what the editor believes the
readers will consider newsworthy. You can tell a lot about the
integrity of a newspaper by what ends up on page one, under
what headline, beside what image.

Editors use a variety of formulas to make their decision, but no
resource counts more than their personal experience, their
"thirty-some years in the journalism business." In other words,
they do not ignore their own sensibilities. Why should they?
They live in the same world as their readers, watch the same TV
commercials, suffer the same charades that pass for politics, and
find themselves in need of an occasional human interest piece to
soften the litany of violence and greed. They've seen cub report-
ers come and go, and they remember all too well that tendency
of the aspiring editorialist to consider every piece a candidate for
the Pulitzer prize. So they listen, with reasonable patience, but
then they decide with a certain fury. Nobody argues. After the
song and dance, the rejects shuffle out, while the winners smile
and head back to the desk to put on the finishing touches. Ideas
came, dressed to kill, performed their best, and then got sent
home—all but a few. Such auditioning and deciding is what
editors call publishing.

The self-persuading preacher calls it the first step in arriving at
a germinal idea. Just as in the board room, a parade of ideas will
appear in the preacher's mind and do their bidding. Some are
distinguished because they sound biblical; others are snappy and
proud because they are the latest and the greatest; still others are
tempting because they are easy and dependable (that sermon
went well three years ago). The paper upon which the sermon is
to be written is *all* page one. There can be no wasted words, no
wasted sentences, no wasted paragraphs. The object is not just to
fill the page, but to distinguish it. The object for the editor is to
want to read his own paper; the object for the preacher is to want
to hear her own sermon.

To stay with the analogy, the preacher must know what the people have been reading about and thinking about—what they need more of, less of. The preacher must remember that people walk ordinary paths to church, not gilded roads lined with theological discourse or laced with existential reflection. Some argued whether to come to church at all, fought about it over burnt toast and screaming kids. Others secretly suspect that all sermons are a scold, or a boast, or a paid political announcement. The preacher must discern the spirits and make the call: What do they need to hear? Which ideas are sermon-worthy? And how can I do unto other ears what I am unwilling to do unto my own? It is this need for personal honesty that led one homiletician to write: "If the minister of the word is to recreate the image of man in every age he must first recreate the image for himself, achieving lucidity in his inner discourse as he considers the Christian revelation of man as a creature made in the image of God, yet finite and sinful."[23] Such lack of "lucid inner discourse" provides us with a new understanding of homiletical plagiarism. Plagiarism is usually defined as the preaching of borrowed manuscripts, the reading of words written by others as if they were written by us. But another form of plagiarism is the complete lack of a personal form. R. E. C. Browne reminds us, "No one can preach in the language of a former generation or in any style that does not belong to him without giving the impression of either his own insincerity or the unreality of his subject."[24]

There was a time when the mouthing of certain words guaranteed that anyone present would at least identify the discourse as a sermon—words like *redemption, salvation, sanctification, justification,* and *stewardship*. But with the loss of the pulpit patron's patience and the dazzling competition of other art forms, the effect of these words is often like that of elevator music: people endure it but are glad to get where they are going.

The self-persuading preacher will not hesitate to give certain words a rest, or retire them altogether. Instead of making people feel guilty because they don't understand King James English, the difficulty of lost meaning will be confessed first by the preacher, whose ears aren't that old either. After all, the fundamental job of interpretation is to make things clear. David Buttrick advises us to "search the language of human conversation and, once more, find images and metaphors to proclaim the gospel. What we cannot do is to fall back on stock theological terminology to any great degree."[25]

In addition to searching the language of human conversation, why not also search our own? The myth continues in rhetoric that we should talk to others the way we think they should be talked to, rather than the way we might talk to ourselves. In using what the ancients called the "grand style," it is often our humanity that suffers. We can be grand by being utterly prosaic, or, abandoning the rhetoric of the Academy because we aren't out to impress ourselves, we can be gentle and colloquial. The fact is, we need to learn the art of formalizing our language based on the rules of intrapersonal communication. Sermons ought to start as heartfelt, unadorned soliloquies, and then get dressed on the way to church.

The word *absurd* comes from the Latin *ab-surdus* meaning "absolutely deaf." To quit listening is to become absurd. On the other hand, *obedience* is from a Latin root, *ob-audiens*, which means "to listen thoroughly." Although this concept is usually applied to the spiritual disciplines, it ought to be applied to preaching as well. One of the most intangible and yet unmistakable qualities of great preaching, is that you can almost hear the preacher listening.

Finally, self-monitored speech is not only considerate but empowering. To witness someone who pays close attention to each and every sound, and reacts as if the stakes are high, is to be given permission to play the same high-stakes game. To listen to someone who rolls certain words around in his mouth as if they were hot on the tongue, or too effervescent to confine, or too amazing not to launch is to learn, by imitation, the spellbinding quality of human speech. The passion of a great preacher causes no small amount of constructive jealousy in the listener. Perhaps, thinks someone in the congregation, if I were to care that much for language, listen that hard, and respond that authentically, I too could move every heart in the house, including my own. For in self-persuasion, unlike in the giving of gifts, it is not just the thought that counts. It is the sound of the thinking.

Chapter 8
The Self-Persuading Preacher and Dialectic

Great Preaching, like great art, cannot be the work of those who know no chaos within them, and it cannot be the work of those who are unable to master the chaos within them. . . . Now as ever, the most searching questions a minister of the Word knows are those which he asks himself.

—R. E. C. Browne

Attitudes and Arguments

If the purpose of preaching is to persuade those listening to believe in the revelations of the Gospel and to manifest such belief in the evidence of their living, then it becomes vitally important to know how and why people change their minds. Because the theory of self-persuasion locates the critical effect within self-generated messages produced by active and involved listeners, the ancient art of dialectic must be carefully considered.

Centuries ago, a philosophical split occurred between classical understandings of the nature and purpose of rhetoric and dialectic. The early treatment of dialectic does not distinguish it from logic: "Rather dialectic or logic is divided on the authority of Cicero into two parts . . . one concerned with judgment, the other . . . concerned with discovery."[1] It was during the period that scholars call the "Christianization of rhetorical thought" that dialectic was subordinated to rhetoric. According to Boethius, dialectic had to do with "thesis," whereas rhetoric was concerned with "hypothesis." Furthermore, although dialectic uses interrogation and response with its arguments set forth in syllogisms, rhetoric uses continuous speech involving enthymemes: "the end of dialectic is to force what one wishes from an adversary, that of rhetoric to persuade a judge."[2]

This may sound like irrelevant ancient history, but the subordination of dialectic survives to this day as a polite prejudice against the role of dialogue in homiletics. That is, mental combat may prepare the sermon by solidifying a thesis, but once the pulpit light comes on, the fussing stops and the selling begins. The problem here is obvious: the listener never crawls into the ring, and the preacher is reduced to eloquent ringside announcer.

The Greeks believed that a trivium of grammar, dialectic, and rhetoric supported the classic components of a model education. Grammar taught by construction; dialectic expounded by argument; and rhetoric consisted of persuasion.[3] But the categories overlap: this tripod is closer to a spiral. Grammar is more than syntax: the arrangement of words makes a considerable difference in persuasive effect. Dialectic is more than detached debate: dialogue is part of the thinking process itself. And rhetoric is more than a stylized report on the result of the debate. It must preserve the debate and invite the listener to join in.

When Plato first began inventing dialogues for the purpose of allowing students to be drawn vicariously into the experience of philosophical inquiry, he was demonstrating the inseparability of form and content. People are not ultimately persuaded by accepting or rejecting the truth that others have discovered and are now peddling; rather, they are persuaded by their *involvement* in the dialectic of truth-finding. In this sense, self-persuasion is inherently Platonic.

Long before the term *attitude* arose, Plato understood the resistance that human beings display towards being told what to believe or toward any rhetorical strategies that intimidate or coerce. He allowed his students to overhear arguments between the questioning hero, Socrates, and some character who represented a position the teacher sought to modify through dialogue. Thus he created a universal tension: that between our love of the teacher and our love of our own opinions. Acting as midwife, the teacher helps the student to "recall," out of a shared divine repository where pure truth resides, that insight that is already in him but has been blurred by uncritical thinking or obscured by the passions. To teach is to facilitate the removal of obstacles to self-learning.[4]

We have already described the first encounter with a text as "overhearing," and the process of preserving a form that engages the listeners as "remythologizing." Furthermore, we have called the interaction between the preacher and the text a self-persuading "conversation." Another way to say the same thing would be to insist that the sermon does not abandon the very dialectic that created it. Rather, it is an amplified and stylized version of the dialogue between the minister and the essential message of the text. This dialogue takes place in front of and on behalf of those who listen and who, like Plato's student, share in the dialogue by *identifying* with the teacher and recognizing themselves in the universal predicaments of the human condition.

The listeners who walk into a sanctuary and sit before a pulpit carry with them a set of strongly held and carefully guarded opinions formed over a lifetime of sorting out the bombardment of stimuli that we call consciousness, using what psychologists call "cognitive schemata."[5] These mental grids or imaginary templates in the brain help us to sort out and make sense of what would otherwise overwhelm us. We cannot start from scratch every day deciding what is good and bad, right and wrong, beautiful and ugly.

Just as physical health is defined as homeostasis, or a chemical balance, so too must humans have a certain attitudinal stasis— a place to stand, an orientation, a way to make sense of the world. Such attitudes are formed through a lifetime of conversing with what's out there, sorting, judging, and interpreting what happens to us—what we see, do, and feel. Attitudes are not changed quickly, and when they are, it is usually through a process not unlike that which formed them. Just as we have talked ourselves into certain attitudes, we have to talk ourselves out of them.

When Gordon Allport defined attitudes as "a general and enduring positive or negative feeling about some person, object, or issue," he provided several significant insights into the dialectical nature of attitude change. First, the word *general* suggests that although formed over years as a result of specific experiences, attitudes lodge in the brain as a kind of nonspecific residue. Because of this, they may show up as specific behaviors but resist being analyzed in specific ways.

For example, racial prejudice is demonstrated in discrete and observable human actions but resists being talked about in specific and logical ways. The kindly but revealing expression, "Some of my best friends are black!" indicates just how vague and illusive prejudice can be. We are afflicted with it generally, even subconsciously, but we act on it in specific ways that we frequently deny. Many attitudes, especially those born of fear and insecurity, keep themselves hidden in dark places, squinting against the intrusion of an indicting light.

Second, the fact that attitudes are "enduring" is of no small importance to preachers. Attitudes tell us who we are and give us identity and comradeship with the like-minded. Those who counsel, "Never discuss religion or politics" know just how precious core values really are and how jealously we guard them. I. A. Richards understood this when he said that Plato's understanding of dialectic "has nearly always been a fighting word and a technique of overcoming . . . . The Prince of Peace himself accepts this image: 'I come not to send peace but a sword.'"[6] Richards continues:

> In the Western intellectual tradition we are taught to be combative in discussion. Mental brawling is no disgrace. The ethics of the duelist or even of the gangster are acceptable to lovers of wisdom. We feel it no shame to dispute and are proud to be trenchant in debate. We admire attacks even when unprovoked, and have not yet dreamt of any need for an intellectual police to guard self-governing topics from aggression.[7]

It was in arguing with orthodox interpretations that Jesus baited his listeners to join the debate: "You have heard it said, but I say . . ." By teaching in parables, he literally conversed with the world, albeit in a radically different way, and thus equipped his disciples to spar with a whole new vocabulary. The method of teaching was almost always indirect and inherently dialogical. And not because he refused to just "tell it like it is," but because in persuasion, as in discipline, if you spare the dialogue, you spoil the congregation.

Rearranging the Furniture of the Mind

The reader will have to forgive my next homely analogy, but the language of the social sciences is often too slippery and obtuse for my purposes. One can only deal in so much abstraction when it comes to the mysterious workings of the mind, and then the search for a meaningful metaphor becomes urgent. Earlier I spoke of the mind as a gallery hung with images. Now it might be helpful to think of "cognitive schemata," those attitudinal grids that process information for us, as furniture arranged in the rooms of the mind. Contemporary research in persuasion suggests that the furniture gets dusted and rearranged, but the rooms themselves are infrequently altered, and additions are nearly unheard of!

Nevertheless, the days of viewing persuasion as a process over which people have little control are long gone. Human action and persuasive effects are responses to self-created messages and a kind of on-going dialectic between our attitudes and some formidable conversation partner. Arguing with the world, we reshape both our attitudes about it and our perception of it.[8] Let's return to the metaphor of rooms and furniture.

The manner in which people decorate their homes and arrange their intimate, domestic space announces to visitors ahead of time what the level of comfort will be, and often the social agenda as well. Walls covered with art reveal the importance of aesthetics, or a penchant for the conspicuous display of investments. A refrigerator covered with the scribbling of children (papers from school with high marks, or notes of endearment) reveals a tender spot for the accomplishments of the young. A large leather recliner in the center of the den, a chair upon which no one sits but the father, reveals the structure of authority. A formal dining room never used, or magazines arranged on coffee tables as props, reveal an artificial emphasis on culture. People decorate their homes and to all those who enter, things are said before a thing is said. The same is true of attitude formation and change. We decorate the mind, and those who enter that space had better be careful where they sit, what they say, and how they go about complimenting or criticizing our space.

If cognitive schemata are dynamic frameworks for processing information, then "self-schematas" refer to those more intimate inferences we make about who *we* are. They are the "abstracted essence of a person's perception of him or herself."[9] Charles Lord has advanced the intriguing notion that the way we process information about ourselves differs from the way we process information about others because we don't *see* ourselves.

Because of the location of the eye, we have no retinal pictures of ourselves going about daily activities, and thus we must rely on largely verbal representations like, "I'm an honest person," or "I am shy." But the way we view ourselves serves as a powerful cognitive reference point for interpreting all information about others.[10] Therefore, we are unlikely to conclude that someone is fat or physically attractive unless he is fatter or more attractive than we perceive ourselves to be. Similarly, when we conclude that another person is foolish, generous, inconsiderate, or loving, it is rarely because we have some external standard for defining these traits. Rather, it is because we have well-defined conceptions of these traits in ourselves, and we make most inferences about others from this vantage point.

The self-persuading preacher must keep in mind that such precious self-schematas (personal items in the house) cannot be reordered by force—no one breaks into someone's home to rearrange the furniture. So, the self-persuading sermon asks to be invited in by not demanding to be invited in. Wishing not to be left out of conversations about a faith that the church-goer at least ostensibly desires means *accommodating* that conversation. The room may need to be straightened, an extra chair may need to be brought in, or the door may need closing, given the private nature of the talk. But every conversation changes the room in which it takes place. Over time, these changes, however slight, change the feeling of the room, and thus, the outlook of the occupant.

The object is to write a sermon that is so authentically and appropriately dialogical that the listeners will want to be part of the conversation. Not because they are being talked to, but because they are being talked about—their doubts, their frustrations, their confusion, their lack of faith is understood intuitively by the preacher. He knows that to move into a certain room in our metaphorical house of being is to respect what kind of conversation can take place there, and how best to invite us in: attics are for memories, kitchens for gossip, dens for the signing of contracts and the drawing of wills, and rec rooms for loud jokes, instant replays, and exaggerated tales of athletic prowess. The sermon that can move into a room and rearrange it, or just leave it in a different humor, is a sermon that knows how to make the conversation partners believe that *they* are responsible for the new design.

Dialectic is the art of contagious conversation. It is not made up of grand, sweeping statements about what we "ought to do," "must do," or "should do." It has the sound of something that can carry its own weight, make its own case, call attention to itself effortlessly. It is about real life, real questions, and real feelings captured in authentic dialogue. There is no need to be a hortatory faucet, gushing forth edicts about world hunger. The self-persuading preacher need only describe the sound of a woman in her suburban castle, scraping enough food off the dinner plates and into the garbage disposal to feed a whole family, saying, "I just don't know what to do to get those kids to eat."

Dialectic is not an optional sermon strategy for the self-persuading preacher, because in the classic sense, it is the conversational mirror through which we see ourselves, locate our speaking parts, and find our own lines to say. When Plato described the process of dialectic, he sketched a process remarkably similar to what we are exploring: dialectic opens with a question on an important matter of knowledge or being, defines appropriate terms, presents a response that sets forth hypotheses that are developed through demonstration, opens to healthy debate and refutation, and ends with a modification of the original position held by each partner in the conversation. The result is shared meaning and enlarged understanding.[11]

Although preaching as self-persuasion is considerably more than dialectic adapted to theological purposes, many of the same principles apply. Listeners are entangled more than taught, and participation is not optional. Enlightenment is a continuous process of being drawn into conversation between assumptions, states of being, current attitudes, values, beliefs, morals, and some formidable ideological partner. The purpose is not to win or lose, agree or disagree, but to join the conversation. Talk is almost always symptomatic of change.

Having a Talk with Ourselves about It

The mysteries of the relationship between thought and action, the subjective world of attitudes and opinions, and the incestuous relationship between language and experience all combine to make the concept of self-persuasion seem hopelessly ambiguous, if not scientifically suspicious. It is easy to understand the appeal of more orthodox notions about rhetoric, where speeches could be judged pleasing, effective, or successful. But how are we to measure the effect of people talking to themselves? In fact, how do we even know whether an "intrapersonal" conversation takes place, much less if it is caused by some external agent like a sermon?

Perhaps we should start with the fact that people do indeed talk to themselves, and there must a reason that corresponds to what we know about language and consciousness. If talking is very much like thinking aloud, and thinking is very much like talking to oneself, then any attempt to separate thought and language becomes a rather useless form of philosophical speculation. Talking to oneself is evidence of the performative power of language, where words actually produce the effect they describe. We need to hear ourselves thinking, rehearse our ideas, and overhear our attitudes.

That fact that people insist on hearing themselves say what it is they believe, or question themselves by soliloquy, or encourage themselves by verbalizing positive suggestions is proof that, in a sense, all deliberation culminates in one form of dialectic or another. So strong is the need to converse that if there is not a partner present we will make an audience of ourselves. Social learning theorists explain such behavior as "cognitive consistency."[12] To maintain consistency, we view the world through our very own attitudinal rose-colored glasses. We see what we want to see and hear what we want to hear. And when we get messages that contradict our beliefs or do not reinforce our present attitudes, we very often "have a talk with ourselves about it."

In other words, we all handle dissonance through intrapersonal dialectic. The Scriptures contain numerous examples of what happens when new and radically different notions about righteousness make trouble for those who follow Jesus: "Then some of the scribes said to *themselves*, 'This man is blaspheming'" (Matt. 9:3; emphasis added). "But there were some who said to *themselves* indignantly, 'Why was this ointment thus wasted?'" (Mark 14:4 RSV; emphasis added). "The Pharisees and their scribes were *complaining* to his disciples, saying, 'Why do you eat and drink with tax collectors and sinners?'" (Luke 5:30; emphasis added). "But they were filled with fury and *discussed* with one another what they might do to Jesus" (Luke 6:11; emphasis added).

In a sense, much of the Bible is a record of the dissonance created when new religious insights, revelations, or definitions forced the listeners to resolve the discrepancies by either adopting the new order or actively resisting it. In other words, the Scriptures are full of faith arguments. Some are soliloquies, as in the book Job: "Does God pervert justice?" Some are symbolic fits of nighttime mumbling, as when Jacob wrestles the angel of God's conscience: "I will not let you go until you bless me." And some are reports of hearts strangely warmed long before Wesley, as when two disciples walked with a stranger on the lonely road to Emmaus: "Did not our hearts burn within us while he talked to us on the road, while he opened to us the scriptures?"

The narratives of Jesus' temptation are supreme examples of gospel dialectic. In the shimmering heat of the desert, mixed with the hallucinations of fasting, various options for ministry come trooping across the stage of his mind, all handsomely dressed and smooth of tongue. As, one by one, Jesus rejects messianic convention, the text preserves one of the most dramatic intrapersonal debates in Scripture. The words of Milton from *Paradise Lost* describe the most frightening journey any one of us will ever take: "Jesus into himself descended."

This is the essential dialectic of faith. This is the way human beings think, act, rethink, and react their way through life. The self-persuading preacher must not forfeit this essential process by engaging in it in the study but dispensing with it in the pulpit. The argument with the text in the study is to be brought forward and preserved in the sermon. It is not unlike the argument that parishioners might have if given the chance—and by preserving the dialectic, they *are* given the chance. The preacher's struggle both invites and legitimizes their struggle.

What the self-persuading preacher knows is that the metaphorical house into which she invites the text for conversation is decorated very much like those of her listeners. The mere presence of some visitors will leave her house changed, and theirs as well. Some will make us uncomfortable, others will get hurried out, but still others will remain long after departing. Some ideas are so radical that we must invite friends over to defend us, or quote famous people to defend the status quo. Some parables are so subversive that their presence seems to shift the whole house, making the once-familiar view suddenly unfamiliar.

The point is, we go on talking long after the visitor has left, and we will be responsible, ultimately, for what we say. If it was all too much to bear, this strange conversation with this strange idea, we will justify our original position: "Like I've always said, you can't just go around loving everybody!" Or, troubled into a new vantage point, we will often try to help ourselves stay there and not retreat: "Come to think of it, I had never thought that the list of the 'unlovable' might include me." What characterizes the good sermon is not some tally at the end of the benediction. No sermon worthy of itself can be shaken off by shaking the preacher's hand. It should have a life beyond the parking lot, intruding upon lunch, or even returning to haunt the deliberations and decisions of the week. The true test is not, "Did you hear such-and-such a sermon?" But, "Have you *spoken* of it since?"

The Sermon as an Irresistible Intruder

The self-persuading sermon comes dressed as a conversation partner, not as so many points to be defended in a sequential monologue of admirable logic. It does not threaten, frighten, or shame the listener into new life. It does not blast the anonymous sins of anonymous people in distant cities that we would secretly like to visit. It comes as an irresistible intruder. It moves over and around us more than it moves toward us—talking with love and urgency about the things that separate us from God. If it tried harder to be noticed, we would probably miss it. Think again about how different dialectic is from rhetoric:

> Rhetoric satisfies the listener, and at the end of a rhetorical presentation, the listener says, "That was a good speech." As a speech it is an identifiable entity, it has form and substance and can be repeated as is or printed and published. Dialectic, however, disturbs a listener toward a kind of conversion of thought or values or life direction, but it proceeds "at its own expense." As it effects an experience in the listener, the presentation itself is used up. [13]

What matters to the self-persuading preacher in the end is not what the listener remembers as having been said in the sermon, but what he remembers of what the sermon caused him to feel and then say. No one lectures, scolds, or frightens someone into an attitude, value, or belief. Rather, such states are the result of having conversed with life and then having learned something from the conversation. Furthermore, there is a desire to continue the conversation, for when communication ceases, then to a great extent so does life.

This is more than navel-gazing existentialism. When the subject is the Gospel, the conversation partners are not just formidable—they can be almost unbearable. To say that a sermon is an irresistible intruder is not necessarily to say that it is pleasant company, but rather that it is a compelling presence. It speaks so directly and so unapologetically to the human condition that one would have to work to ignore it. It is irresistible precisely because it addresses some state of imperfection, arousing in all of us what Kenneth Burke calls "guilt." Because human beings are sensitive to their failings and are able, through language, to imagine a state of perfection, this "principle of perfection," or categorical guilt arises as a result of the discrepancy between the real and the ideal.[14]

Again, this guilt is not about feeling bad, in the conventional sense, nor is it about experiencing loathing or self-pity. It is, for Burke, a very idealistic term, striking at the very heart of the religious impulse. Our separation from God drives the universal impulse of faith, a longing to rejoin what was broken apart, to trigger what theologians these days are calling "primal memory." Augustine expressed it with simple eloquence: "Our hearts are restless until they find rest in Thee."

The self-persuading sermon is an irresistible intruder not because it is easy company or because the talk is small. Rather, it silences what is small, and speaks instead of large and compelling things—so that the level of discourse in the listener can rise accordingly. For this reason, it is vitally important that the sermon not water down the offense of the Scripture as if to cool or strain or make more palatable what lay people could not otherwise handle. Transliteration of difficult words and brief historical-critical remarks are appropriate for understanding context. But the message of the text should never be tranquilized. Nobody picks a fight with a weakling, and no one really wants to converse with a message that has been turned into a bumper sticker.

Again, the idea is that authentic and passionate conversation is contagious. The preacher's level of intensity affects the level of listening and raises the stakes for everyone concerned. It is no accident that when a musical virtuoso performs, the level of music appreciation in the audience rises correspondingly. Often, the listener is not aware of her own *capacity* for Bach until she hears someone engage the score on this level. Walking from the concert hall, the patron often feels compelled to talk about what she heard and in the process begins to sound like a reviewer for the arts page of the newspaper. But she isn't promoting anything. She's just naturally excited about having spent time with Bach.

Preaching as self-persuasion is no less a performance of the biblical score. Rhythms and crescendos exist in language as surely as in music. Melody lines and refrains, serving as they do to both unfold and remind, can be powerfully adapted to preaching. Some verses take us away, others remind us of where we've been. And what makes jazz work holds a lesson for the pulpit: it can never be the same way twice. But the test of good music is that it gets under your skin. It is an irresistible intruder, and you catch yourself humming the tune long after the performance is over.

If the sermon is to be heard and new conversations are to be sparked, then the intruder will have to be more than beguiling— it will also have to be wise to the workings of the human mind. For example, sometimes it is very effective for a preacher to employ what persuasion theorists call *counter-attitudinal* messages, intentionally stating an opinion or belief that is the opposite of what they really believe. In order to get the listener to identify honesty with the enormous distance separating us from the demands of the Gospel, the preacher becomes the antagonist, much after the fashion of the dialectic of C. S. Lewis. To listen as a preacher actually creates dissonance is often very liberating to a congregation, especially if they are used to hearing him endlessly observe the world from over the shoulder of Jesus.

In the sanctuary, there is also a kind of group-think going on. Listeners repeatedly evaluate how responsible and appropriate their own opinions and attitudes are. This process, called social comparison theory, is based on our tendency to want to use groups of "similar others" to define social reality.[15] In such cases, the sermon not only intrudes but reassures, especially if the listener can identify with the preacher's struggle and participate in appropriating the results.

Yet another contemporary persuasion theory with important implications for preaching is called social learning theory. It maintains that people adjust their behavior in terms of "continuous reciprocal interaction" among overt behaviors, the perceived positive or negative consequences of that behavior, and people's internal cognition and emotions. The essence of all human learning, according to Albert Bandura, is a search for "if-then" relationships. If a person behaves (believes) in a certain way, then what will be the consequences?[16]

All these so-called active participation models of persuasion preserve elements of choice, imitation, and self-monitoring. And the if-then construct is essentially another name for the process of dialectic. If one is going to take the Sermon on the Mount seriously, then what is one to make of our increasingly Roman culture, where men and women mutilate themselves in search of the perfect body? If Luke's church was the original Rainbow Coalition, why are so many birds of a feather flocked together in our churches? If wealth is spiritually debilitating, why has the breeding of money become a national obsession?

The self-persuading preacher duels with Scripture because reconciling *if* and *then* is the business of healing a broken world. Just as the text came first into the study as an irresistible intruder, compelling the preacher to conversation, so does the sermon come into the sanctuary as an irresistible intruder. Born as dialectic, it survives as dialectic on the way to the pulpit, and its final act is to create in the listener the very dialectic it embodies. Remember, it was not a discussion group that Jacob was hosting by the banks of the Jabbok River. Nor was it a resolution that he issued at sunrise. It was a wrestling match, and when the sun came up he was called by a different name, and he was limping. So much for "meek and mild, gentle as a child."

Cognitive Dissonance and Grace

It is the nature of dialectic to make choices available, not to coerce or manipulate their selection. A sermon that preserves the quality of dialectic will not necessarily be a fictitious dialogue, in the Platonic sense, but it will have the quality of dialogue and the tone of conversation. The nature of the Gospel is such that the relationship between the self-persuading preacher and the essential message of the text will be like that between the sailors of old and the mythical siren songs. Compelled toward a text that may very well sink him, the preacher takes the risk in order to hear the song and to sing it. His conversations are both compulsive and dangerous.

Because he lives in the same world as his congregation, influenced by its wisdom and its illusions, there will be conflicts in the conversation, painful moments when cherished assumptions are battered, shortfalls exposed, and hypocrisies of the human condition made to squint and scurry under the searchlight of the Gospel. There is no escaping participation in the experience of judgment and grace that will accompany every genuine act of self-persuasion. The Gospel causes dissonance. The manner in which it is reduced, balancing the gentleness of a healthy self-respect with the judgment that all personal growth requires, will set the tone for the listener to do likewise.

In 1957, a sociologist named Leon Festinger pioneered the theory of cognitive dissonance, arguing that human beings desire consistency of cognition in their psychological world. When our behavior does not match our beliefs, it short-circuits our attitudinal wiring, causing dissonance.[17] For example, a person who smokes cigarettes knows that this behavior is in a dissonant relationship with the knowledge that smoking causes disease and death. Telling a lie creates dissonance within a person who believes that she is honest. "White lies," such as telling the hostess of a boring party that it was an enchanted evening, do not create dissonance because social pressures to be polite take precedence over what would be a harmful kind of honesty. Whenever *genuine* dissonance is created, however, people want to eliminate it, bringing cognition and behavior into harmony. In other words, something has to give. Either the behavior changes, the cognition changes, or some way of justifying the dissonance is found.

The Gospel, once called The Great Offense, is bound to create dissonance in anyone who honestly engages it. The prophet Hosea married a known prostitute and then patiently kept the light on, night after self-destructive night, as a way of describing the nature of true love, not to mention what it would be like to be God, married to us. Jesus almost gets killed after preaching his inaugural sermon in his home synagogue, calls some of the most respected pillars of society a "brood of vipers," and declares that some of the lost and the least stand a better chance of getting into the kingdom than those who are certain they hold a ticket.

Some of the parables are not just surprising; they are shocking. One describes a group of men who work only one hour and get paid as much as a group who worked all day. Their generous employer gets in trouble not because he *mis*treats, but because he *over*treats. Another parable describes a group of bridesmaids who slumber before a late wedding, forgetting to keep oil in their lamps. When the party finally begins, they ask to borrow some oil but no one shares. Then they ask to be admitted to the feast, but the door is slammed in their faces. Could it be, that in the vocabulary of God, there is the word "no," as well as the word "yes?"

The most familiar of all parables describes an irresponsible and indulgent son who takes his inheritance early and blows it on wine, women, and song. While his brother stays behind to mend fences and keep the farm, his father throws a party for the prodigal son upon his return. Who can blame the older brother for being a little miffed? There is no lecture, no probation period, not even a line like, "Do you know how disappointed your mother and I have been?" Just unbridled joy and feasting, for what was dead now lives, and what was lost is now found. No wonder Ernest Campbell said that the biggest problem with American Christianity is that we have a Loving Father Gospel in an Elder Brother church.

In many ways, the Scriptures are the voice of a vocal, even eccentric minority. They call a silent and ethically bankrupt majority to task for their complicity in oppression and injustice. They call the rituals of organized religion empty and pretentious. Now the self-persuading preacher finds herself a part of the majority, the spiritual leader of the world's largest religion. Conservative preachers consider the faith to be anything *but* subversive; they call it the last, best hope for a return to traditional family values. Even though its founder was penniless and was tried and executed as a subversive and a blasphemer, the Gospel is now largely the property of the wealthy and the powerful. In the United States, most preachers are called upon to preach to the rich, and to quote a man whose patience with organized religion was thin and whose approach to faith was distinctly antitemple. In fact, preachers find themselves in a proprietary position in the midst of a vast ecclesiastical bureaucracy that might well be the object of Jesus' scorn were Jesus to return among us.

The point of all this is that dissonance must not be avoided, as if in church "never is heard a discouraging word and the skies are not cloudy all day." The last thing a self-persuading preacher should do is "shed his sickness," as D. H. Lawrence would say. Both a longing for and a long list of complaints against the Gospel should be the stuff of the pulpit. The way in which a preacher reduces his own dissonance, not somebody else's, acts as a model to those who listen and want more than advice. In this sense, preaching is not just an activity. It is a behavior.

Reducing dissonance usually occurs in one of three ways: either the cognition is denied, which is often dishonest; the behavior is recanted, which can make a fiction of preaching; or the attitude is altered. Obviously, preaching as self-persuasion aims at the third option, but this is no easier for the one who is talking than it is for the one who is listening. What we must remember is that one is asked to call oneself a Christian long before becoming one. Odd as it may sound, we must first pretend to believe by hearing ourselves say what we may not yet believe. After all, it is in being compelled to kindness that one becomes kind; it is in the act of being hesitantly generous that one becomes genuinely generous; and it is in acting the part of the compassionate one that we become truly compassionate. In other words, the final act of grace is to make a person gracious.

Role-Playing Our Way to Faith

One of the benefits of dialectic is that by choosing parts in a conversation with Scripture or with ourselves, we mentally rehearse a role that we might otherwise be unwilling or unable to act out. This freedom and distance allow us to literally overhear ourselves talking as we wish we could. Acting the part, rhetorically, often causes a transformation of which the actor is unaware. We have already mentioned that Broadway actors often have difficulty separating their real lives from the parts they play, especially if the show runs for years. But this problem is really testimony to a fundamental fact of human nature: we grow into faith over a lifetime. It is the residue of a thousand hymns, the imprint of the melody of Scripture, and the discipline of repeating the words of life until they seep into our very soul that makes us Christian, if anything can.

To say that the self-persuading preacher acts is not to say that it is all make-believe, only that it is a role beyond his capacity. The preacher also wants help with his unbelief. If he did not believe that playing the part could stretch one into the part, then we would call his acting a charade. As it is, we call it self-persuasion.

How else could it be? Faith is not a static thing but a journey, and the preacher also wants to go further. In the development of faith, as in the experience of buying a new outfit, some things must be tried on before they are purchased. After all, the expense and the altered image of this new look are just too significant. So the preacher acts the role of reckless companion and mirrors the new look for us. She is the subversive, the spendthrift, the alter-ego that says, "Perhaps it's me." She is a bad influence in a good way. It is more dangerous to go shopping with her than to go shopping alone. Her enthusiasm is contagious.

Role-playing involves mentally placing oneself in the position of another who is faced with a specific set of circumstances (in this case, understanding and appropriating the text). By experiencing the consequences of that other's behavior, we learn what might happen to us in similar circumstances. Psychotherapists first employed role-playing in the 1950s as a learning technique called "psychodrama."[18] Adolescents with hostile feelings toward a parent, for example, would role-play happy individuals. The results indicated changed attitudes on the part of the teenagers and an appreciation of the positive consequences of realistic optimism on the part of those who were depressed.[19]

However uncomfortable some clergy feel about their status as role models, there is no escaping the fact that in the sanctuary, they are the Significant Person, and their behavior *will* be modeled. Sooner or later, congregations are shaped by the extended personality of their ministers. It is their precision with language that transforms ordinary listeners into demanding and discriminating listeners. It is their appetite for engaging current events in a context appropriate to the Gospel that raises the political and social awareness of those who listen. It is their sense of urgency about the message, their attention to form, their respect for the spoken word, and their reactions to what they hear themselves saying that advances all these dispositions in the congregation. In other words, playing the role of a disciplined and imaginative preacher advances the same qualities in the listener that it demonstrates in the speaker.

If this is not authentic, if the preacher is writing prescriptions that exclude his own illnesses or making thunder where there is no lightning, then the process breaks down and becomes a forgery. On the other hand, research indicates that when role-playing is personally relevant, the actor will verbalize about the consequences to a far greater extent.[20] This means that those self-generated messages so crucial to self-persuasion must be a natural, unself-conscious part of the preacher's lead role: talking to the text, to himself, and to the congregation whose situation he knows as intimately as his own.

Role-playing is not an exercise in deception. It is not an attempt on the part of the preacher to be something that he isn't. It is rather an attempt to become something more than he is. The operating assumption is that when it comes to the Gospel we are all walking around a mountain too high to climb. The preacher is not issuing reports from the top but keeping us company on the climb. Richard Weaver suggests that preachers remember Plato, but long for God:

> What Plato has prepared us to see is that the virtuous rhetorician, who is a lover of truth, has a soul of "such" movement that its dialectical perceptions are consonant with those of a divine mind. . . . The good soul, consequently, will not urge a perversion of justice as justice in order to impose upon the commonwealth. Insofar as the soul has its impulse in the right direction, its definitions will agree with the true nature of intelligible things.[21]

The posture of the self-persuading preacher is as gatekeeper to the common house of faith. Inviting a steady stream of characters from the Bible into the living room, sitting down with ideas overheard in stories and notes jotted from Proverbs, shaken by parables, moved by the melody of Psalms, stirred by farewell speeches, riled by deceit, and softened by human tenderness, the preacher not only converses with all these things, he lets them roam the whole house. He is suspicious of some, incredulous towards others. Some seem embarrassed to be out of place, others seem right at home.

Were it not for the deadline of the Sunday morning service, he might never have started what he is forced to finish. But he is encouraged by the fact that no one walks into the pulpit with a fever who is not a little bit contagious. The time has come to turn our attention to the reasons why passion breeds passion. Why is it that self-persuasion creates empathy without having to engineer it? What is it about authentic human drama that compels imitation? Why has no one ever discussed the most elemental force at work when humans witness pain and joy, pleasure and sorrow, grief and wonder? Why is the word *vicarious* not at the heart of the evangelism of preaching?

Chapter 9
The Self-Persuading Preacher and Vicariousness

Communication takes place when one mind so acts upon its environment that another mind is influenced, and in that other mind an experience occurs which is like the experience in the first mind, and is caused by that experience.

—I. A. Richards

The Roots of Human Empathy

T. S. Eliot reputedly said that the purpose of literature is to turn blood into ink. Charles Bartow, a Presbyterian minister and homiletics professor, has added a coda: "If that is true (Eliot's metaphor), and I believe it is, and if it further is true that sermons may be thought of as a specific type of literature . . . then it is the purpose of speaking that sermonic literature to turn the ink back into blood."[1] The self-persuading preacher does not traffic in borrowed energy; instead she speaks from passion to passion, listening not just to what she heard the text say, but also to what she hears herself saying about it. She must be what Bartow calls a "listening preacher." In fact, the professor strikes at the heart of our discussion when he asks this question: "How do you talk so that others can hear you listening?"[2]

The answer is simple at the surface but baffling and complex at the level of implementation. To become an unself-conscious model of self-persuasion is not something that a good course or two can provide or some directed readings can explain. It is an art cultivated out of a basic belief in the emphatic nature of human emotions, and the paradoxical belief that genuine passion is *affective* without intention. That is, we do not necessarily need a rhetorical strategy to arouse emotion in others so much as we need a rhetorical strategy to exhibit the authentic emotions in ourselves.

We know from the earliest experiments with children that empathic emotions and vicarious learning experiences make it possible to learn much faster than by individual trial and error. What psychologists call modeling behavior is a powerful teacher. Such modeling and the imitative behavior that results from it are especially keen in an atmosphere of intimacy and trust—first with a parent or parents, and later with admired role models. In the ministry, the congregation gradually soaks up and emulates the extended personality of the minister. On a regular basis, preaching is the principal form of emotional, intellectual, and spiritual self-disclosure. It is a form of parenting through empathy.

The roots of such empathy are sunk deep in the formative consciousness of children. Any observant parent has watched a brother and sister quarrel endlessly, teasing, nagging, even inventing games to make one another miserable. But let one of them cut a finger, and something else happens, something which seems out of character amidst all this belligerence. The one who is not injured will volunteer to go for the band-aid and will show immediate and genuine concern, especially if there is blood. Suffering brings a universal empathic response, even if the afflicted is one's "worthless, stupid" brother or sister! Where does this underlying tenderness come from?

It comes from an innate, vicarious identification with the emotional states of others. We learn vicariously, feel vicariously, even adopt value structures vicariously. But first, we must be aroused, and that vicarious arousal is not triggered unless we observe a genuine emotional state in others: "People commonly display emotional reactions while undergoing rewarding or painful experiences. Observers are easily aroused by such emotional expressions . . . vicarious arousal is an integral aspect of human empathy."[3] This experience is not to be confused with sympathy, which is often mixed with feelings of pity—an emotion that can masquerade as compassion but is basically self-serving. Empathy has to do with actually *feeling* what someone else feels. It is a powerful, innate form of identification born of common human experience. There is not an adult capable of remembrance who does not recall an injury on the playground, arriving on the scene of an accident before the ambulance, or the physical pain that comes just from watching a friend fall, break a bone, or be publicly humiliated or embarrassed. Just watching another child struggle to give the right answer in class turned our cheeks hot and sent waves of panic through our bodies. It is a kind of psychosomatic wince. Yawning is contagious. But so are tears; so are anger, jealousy, and joy. We seek the company of the optimistic and the self-confident because some of it rubs off, and we avoid the surly, the contemptuous, and the depressed for the same reason. There are people who can change a room just by walking into it. They have "presence," we say, but in fact we are picking up their emotional states vicariously. One of the qualities of leadership is the ability to disseminate a vision and make it contagious. For the self-persuading preacher this means that no heat can be expected where there is no fire.

In a sense, what children discern in the case of injury is not forsaken in adulthood. Emotional states that result from the unexpected or the unavoidable plight strike a responsive chord in all of us. The large and common forces in life—pain, confusion, curiosity, anger, embarrassment, fear, desire, insecurity, vulnerability, ecstasy, and the like—all draw us into unavoidable empathic response. When we sense that others are genuinely victimized by the plight of being human, we feel vicariously victimized as well. Manufactured tears do not move us; real tears cannot help but move us.

Self-persuasion rests on the authority of self-generated messages arising out of authentic emotions. The danger of fraudulent emotions can therefore hardly be understated. If one learns the art of crying on cue, then the tears in the congregation will have a corresponding artificiality. There is a big difference between wallowing in tears and occasionally fighting them back. Augustine knew that emotionally honest preaching breeds emotionally honest responses. The listener will be persuaded,

if he be drawn by your promises, and awed by your threats;
if he reject what you condemn, and embrace what you com-

mend; if he grieve when you heap up objects for grief, and rejoice when you point out an object for joy; if he pity those whom you present to him as objects of pity, and shrink from those whom you set before him as men to be feared and shunned.[4]

Vicariousness is a phenomenon that requires the immediacy of human presence. For this reason, televised preaching, powerful and seductive though it is, can never replace what is truly live— the congregation. The Book of Exodus catches the significance of the ethos of personal encounter in any "humane" communication: "And God spoke unto Moses face to face as a man speaks to a friend" (33:11 RSV).

Surely this is the ultimate expression of intimacy, so much so that the idea that anyone has ever seen God face to face is elsewhere rejected. To "look someone in the eye" is regarded as a test of honesty precisely because the face so unself-consciously betrays the emotions. Gifted storytellers will confess that their facial expressions are mirrored in listeners, who would be uncomfortable if they knew the extent to which they were reciprocating.

Again, this is how theater works. Kenneth Burke was correct when he said, "In its simplest manifestation, style is ingratiation."[5] No one on stage stops to order the audience in or suggest that it would be appropriate to shed a tear just now. The action proceeds oblivious to the audience even though it has been rehearsed and crafted on behalf of the audience. Preaching as self-persuasion operates by the same empathic indirectness.

The experience of conversing with a text or its germinal idea is inescapably personal. Unless the preacher is proof-texting, or co-opting Scripture for a predetermined agenda, the conversation will be humane and idiosyncratic. This does not mean the final sermon will be a private affair, where all in attendance feel like aural voyeurs. It means that passion, by nature, is not something we conjure, whip up, or borrow. It is something born of an abiding belief in the importance of what we are doing, and a conviction that the spirit is present in both the impulse to speak and in the completion of speech. The best advice to offer the self-persuading preacher sounds almost flippant: get real.

Sermonic Passion: Where Does It Come From?

The fundamental premise underlying our view of the contagious nature of human emotions is that *impression* precedes *expression*. A trip to the pulpit without genuine passion is not only an exercise in futility but in deception as well. Why should we expect listeners to get excited about something that doesn't excite us? If the sermon is to be a consummate act of self-persuasion, then the preacher must locate and be honest about what is worthy of persuasion. The conversation with the text should be more formative than worthwhile, and more germinal than useful. After all, the listener has a right to witness change, not just hear about it. And the preacher has the responsibility to speak as one who cannot help but speak, even though, as R. E. C. Browne has written: "Every significant utterance is a wound."[6]

At the heart of this description of meaningful rhetoric as painful is the knowledge that we do not speak to the depths unless we have plumbed them. Pedantic speech from the pulpit invariably comes from a preacher's life, pedantically lived. Sermons that roll along, content to prove the obvious and avoid the mysterious, create listeners that are both simple-minded and paranoid. A preacher who is unafraid to jump into deep water creates a congregation that does more than tread water. One thing is certain: passion will show upon a preacher's face. It will leak around and through his habits of speech as surely as a flashlight smothered in a child's hand shines right through the flesh.

Walter Ong has reminded us that the spoken word has a unique capacity to reveal what he calls our "interiority."[7] That is, lacking true impression, the voice will betray the absence. Ironically, the very origin of the term *proof-texting* is the mistaken notion that the text serves an *evidential* as opposed to a germinal function. If there is no real curiosity aroused, no delight in discovering a relevant word or idea, no amazement at hearing a clear message across the ages, no indictment at feeling personally judged, no joy at feeling personally inspired, then it is a fundamental act of dishonesty to climb the pulpit stairs expecting the text to do for others what it could not do for you.

Again we hear Burke with profit: "Style is an attempt to 'gain favor' by the hypnotic or suggestive process of 'saying the right thing.'"[8] What can he mean by "hypnotic" and "suggestive" but the compulsions of empathic listening that we are describing? In what social scientists call "vicarious emotional learning," there is evidence that not only are emotions experienced vicariously but attitudes can be *learned* vicariously: "What gives significance to vicarious influence is that people can acquire enduring attitudes and emotional dispositions toward things associated with the model's arousal. They learn to fear the things that frightened models, to dislike what repulsed them, and to enjoy what pleased them."[9]

This is one reason why the self-persuading preacher must be extremely careful not to leave the conversation with the text before having something to say. And not just something the congregation needs to hear, but something the preacher needs to hear. After all, the preacher is most at risk when it comes to overexposure and repetition. It is the preacher who is in constant danger of standing so close to something that he can no longer see it, or worse yet, feel it. As biblical scholars have reminded us, "The language of the New Testament has become so familiar it has lost its edge."[10] What may be required is an approach to the text that preserves a kind of naiveté. Only after allowing the text to speak its first word alone is it appropriate to pull down commentaries and do exegesis. Finally, suggests Paul Ricoeur, the student returns to the text with what is called a "second naiveté"—recovering again the narrative and dialectic nature of the text.[11]

A self-persuading sermon cannot be worked up so much as it must be worked out. This means some sermons should never be preached, whereas others should never be finished. And every sermon ought to be able to survive the asking of the most troubling question of all: Who cares? Robert Frost used to say that his poems began "in delight" and ended "in wisdom." Think how revealing this is from the perspective of self-persuasion. Frost is admitting that impression is refined and amplified through expression, and that the end-product is an enlightened thing beyond the sum of its parts. The feeling comes first, but the feeling is not enough—expression brings maturity to emotions, puts flesh and bones on them, and finally satisfies the poet by giving the poem a life of its own. It leaves home and comes back to teach the teacher.

E. D. Hirsch once described the act of interpretation as a "moment" followed by a "movement"—intuition and precision.[12] The former is what Frost called delight; the latter is what the poet called wisdom. Poems are not finished until the poet performs them. Sermons are not finished until the preacher preaches them. In both cases, the author is indebted to the listener. The reading reminds the author why it was worth the writing, and the empathic listening is a kind of secondary authorship.

To be a self-persuading preacher is to view Scripture as the means by which life is illuminated, not as raw material for the defense of doctrine: "It is not that doctrine is supremely important and that life proves its importance; it is that life is supremely important and doctrine illuminates it."[13] Too often, preachers do not expend the energy necessary to have a bona fide argument with the text. They collect from it more than they converse with it, and the result is feigned passion. No longer really in love with the Gospel, the preacher has nothing much at stake when communicating with it. Content to be partners with the congregation in satisfying one another's basic needs (another Sunday, another dollar), real dialogue fades into a patronizing kind of politeness. Like the death of passion in a marriage, the preacher gets too comfortable with ideas that once seduced him and now merely serve him. Sermons become fortune cookies (fits everyone, applies to no one). For a good example of this emotional mediocrity, listen to a man introduce the wife he no longer loves at a party. "Better half," "bride of my dreams," and "love of my life" may be compensation for the fact that he has forgotten the color of her eyes.

In preaching, lack of conviction has a distinct sound. It is flat, distant, and hollow. But when the preacher has something to say, the effect is no less audible. The conversation that began as a whisper is becoming a shout, and the joy of putting words together is not just a private pastime serving a future eloquence; rather it is for the purpose of consummating private passion in a public hearing, an event where both the risks and rewards are greater than those of solitude.

The truth of what people say "depends on the depth of their engagement rather than the height of their detachment."[14] The very concept of self-persuasion demands engagement and rejects detachment. There can be no artificial separation of what is good for people from what is good for the preacher. What is true in the jargon of computers is true of the pulpit: junk in, junk out. What was missing at the beginning cannot be created in the end, except by artificial means. Whether our thought is dominated by the left brain or right brain, we cannot persuade out of an emotional void. Remember, we continue to confuse emotion with emotionalism:

> Some of us have been educated to regard emotion negatively, to define it as disorganized behavior or a biological lag. In the wake of this perspective came a view of maturity that was without emotion. The mature person served afternoon tea to both teams but certainly never got caught up in the struggle. The result was a tourist-class citizen, negotiating life with a calm indifference, preferring to die curled up on some principle rather than give his life fighting for what might eventually be judged an error.[15]

We circle back once again to our original premise: there is no persuasion without passion. And there is no passion without personal involvement. If self-persuasion depends upon the authority of self-generated messages, then the preacher must model this behavior in the pulpit. The preacher cannot be exempt, by design or by the tragic loss of enthusiasm, from the sermon preached. Otherwise, the sermon is a dutiful ecclesiastical delivery—and faith can't be delivered. It can only be demonstrated.

The Power of Preaching Side-by-Side

The deadliest form of preaching is the detached monologue, where advice is offered to help us in general with what, in general, is wrong with us. Since congregations have nothing at all "generally" wrong with them, its members can only sit patiently and receive equal measures of guilt and generic wisdom. The preacher does not talk *with* them, much less *to himself*. And the listener never thinks to respond with messages of his own because the whole experience is light years distant from anything resembling a conversation.

Part of the problem can be blamed on the arrangement of the room, of course. In all but the most modern sanctuaries, the pulpit is still elevated above the pews, bathed in floodlight, ornately thronelike. It does not appear to be the place where one person would stand to have a conversation. Rather it resembles what over time it has become: the place of the Elevated Edict. Reuel Howe writes:

> The preacher looks down; the people look up. Often, as the lights in the church are turned down and a spotlight turned on the preacher, the congregation disappears into an identity-hiding gloom. The elevation of the pulpit lifts the Word of God above life, and would seem to contradict the concept of its embodiment in the life of the people. The arrangement, moreover, confirms the stereotype of the relation between clergy and laity in which the Word is removed from the people and made the preacher's exclusive sphere of responsibility.[16]

Fortunately, the self-persuading preacher can overcome these stereotypes in ways that go far beyond rearranging the furniture. What has been overheard in the text is interpreted and amplified in the sermon. If the congregation senses that the sermon is on their behalf, and not just for their own good, then the preacher's struggle will become the congregation's struggle vicariously, long before any defense mechanisms are erected against agreement. Opinions are easy to reject; struggles are disarming.

Many young preachers could have been spared the turmoil and rejection that accompanies prophetic preaching if only, instead of denouncing, demanding, and standing over against the congregation, they had struggled along side of, and as a true member of, their own congregations. By confessing the difficulty of turning the other cheek, walking the second mile, or loving the unlovable, the self-persuading preacher simultaneously relieves and energizes the congregation. Relief comes in the form of identification (our preacher is not an alien life form); energy comes by virtue of the empathy that mutual struggle creates. In other words, the listeners see faith struggle *validated*.

Odd as it may sound, preachers ought to join the congregations they preach to and think very seriously about what it would be like to have to listen to themselves on a regular basis. It would be a powerful antidote to arrogance, and it would post a vigilant sentinel against creeping condescension. Side-by-side preaching is crucial for self-persuasion in several ways. First, because it levels the playing field and breaks down the barriers that separate the world of lay people from the world of clerics. Second, because it demonstrates that the subject matter is important enough to deserve mutual struggle. And third, because not only can the struggle be modeled vicariously, but the internal standards that drive the dialectic can over time be appropriated through repeated exposure.

Social scientists calls this phenomenon "vicarious motivators," and although it seems at first to have nothing to do with preaching in the conventional sense, it has everything to do with preaching as self-persuasion:

> As people engage in activities they express, from time to time, reactions to their own behavior according to their personal standards. They react self-approvingly when their behavior matches or surpasses their standards but self-critically when it falls short or violates their internal standards. Through repeated exposure to modeled self-reactions, observers eventually extract the underlying standards and often use them as guides for future behavior. [17]

It would be hard to imagine a more important statement about self-persuasion than this. "Through repeated exposure to modeled self-reactions" (the congregation listening week after week to a self-persuading preacher), "observers eventually extract the underlying standards" (vicariously appropriate what drives the preacher to engage the text in certain ways), "and often use them as guides for their own future behavior" (find themselves talking to and about the text like the preacher). Moved by his conversation, he not only encourages their own but teaches them how.

Perhaps it is important here to insert some reassurance about the place of resolution, or affirmation, in the sermon. To say that a self-persuading sermon preserves an authentic struggle and offers it in a sermon whose posture is side-by-side does not mean that the listener is left perpetually without a decision, wandering around perplexed, confused, and sensing that every pulpit bout ends in a split decision. What is meant is that the struggle itself will not be separated from its outcome. Nor will the decision be anyone's private property.

Preaching as self-persuasion is like the layers of the proverbial onion, peeled away to reveal an unending compression of the forces of human communication. Interacting vicariously with the text, the preacher hopes for the same vicarious interaction from the congregation. But the sermon itself is something more than just an opportunity for the listeners. It is also the final act in the self-persuasion of the preacher, when all the preparation, all the listening, and all the revisions culminate in the hearing of the sermon as it was meant to be heard—wrapped in the liturgy, spoken among loved ones, and offered as an act of faith.

If all this sounds like passion breeding passion, it is exactly that. If the preacher is devoted to interpreting Scripture, it will show; if she is devoted to shaking the ancient tree of wisdom until it bears contemporary fruit, it will show; if she is devoted to the creation of sermons that are worthy of everyone's time, including her own, it will show. What sounded good in the study will sound even better in the sanctuary. What she spoke alone to herself gains momentum as it waits to be spoken to many— echoing down the corridors of intimacy and trust, lighting the faces of those she loves, changing their countenance as unselfconsciously as it changes her own. There is a remarkable energy released when people listen intently. There are moments in the sanctuary during a powerful sermon when the listening could break a glass. The harder the congregation listens, the harder the preacher listens. The harder the preacher listens, the harder it is for the congregation not to.

Creating Listeners: A Pygmalion Rhetoric

Let us step back a moment and remember how we got here. At the heart of the theory of self-persuasion is the notion that our own messages carry more weight than those generated by others. Preaching as self-persuasion literally involves getting people to talk to themselves in particular ways by modeling such self-persuasion in the pulpit and thereby triggering a vicarious experience in the listener. We have already mentioned how crucial it is that the entire sermonic experience be conversational, and that the preacher use and understand dialectic. But there are even more specific ways to talk about how this interactive process takes place.

One particular stylistic device used to help create active and imitative listeners is what might be called, for lack of any existing term, a *pygmalion rhetoric*. The term gets its meaning from the famous educational experiment in which teachers were told that a group of randomly selected students had been identified as exceptionally bright, and that they could expect superior achievement from them. The results of the experiment indicated that although none of the students fit the description to begin with, the expectation of superior achievement helped to create such achievement. Interacting with students as if they were exceptional helped to make them so—a kind of self-fulfilling prophecy. Expectations on the part of the teachers manifested themselves in concrete behaviors toward the children—verbal clues, extra attention, and positive feedback. Sensing what was sensed about them, the students literally outdid themselves.

This very same technique can be employed rhetorically to create better listeners. Gifted speakers have been frequently heard to lace their speech with indirect compliments regarding their listener's sensitivity and mental capacity. These comments, usually in the form of an "aside," leave the impression that careful listening is going on, even if it isn't. All this requires is the projection of an internal dialectic onto the listeners as a way of baiting them. For example, skillful preachers, as they track a controversial idea or move into sensitive waters, will often pause to place the polemic in the mouth of the listener: "Now I know what you're thinking . . ." or "Your mind has no doubt raced far ahead of mine to ask the obvious question . . ." or "If you're anything like me, this is no simple matter. You find yourself at odds here, just as I do."

Sometimes a conversational preacher can make a participant of the listener despite the listener's best effort not to listen. Anticipating and then complimenting responses that may not yet have occurred, the preacher creates what he hopes for—and the recipient of the compliment wears it as comfortably as an old sweater. If someone tells me that I am listening keenly, imaginatively, even obstinately, then who am I to argue with the assessment? The assumption that a person is listening, followed by a compliment based on the assumption, becomes an accurate description of how one in fact *is* listening. In self-persuasion, the preacher listens carefully first, and then creates listeners who are equally involved.

The idea that rhetorical style not only produces something worth listening to but also contributes to the listening itself is worth pondering. The clever teacher projects a confidence in students that is invariably rewarded. A gifted preacher can accomplish the same thing by projecting high listening standards upon the congregation until those standards are adopted unaware. Remember Bartow's query: "How can you talk in such a way that others can hear you listening?" One way would be to give everyone in the room *your* ears, to assume that they are listening with the care and urgency that you demonstrate, and in so doing teach them to listen vicariously. Listening as carefully as you do cannot help but lead your audience to speak more carefully too.

We are talking here about something essentially pastoral. It is difficult to overstate the importance of listeners who believe that they are believed in, held up, valued, and taken into serious account from the beginning of the sermon to the end. Plato spoke of this in his metaphor of the speaker as a noble lover who looked upon his audience "not as they were but as they were capable of becoming."[18] Aristotle touched on the same theme when he described a friend as one who wishes for another what he would want for himself.[19] In the unfolding intimacy that is marriage, the participants create each other. After many years, husbands and wives even look similar. The same is true in preaching. Love, intimacy, the exchange of ideas—it all creates a kind of adaptive reciprocity. Sobering as it may sound, our preaching creates the kind of listeners it deserves.

It is not a contradiction to claim that preaching as self-persuasion is listener centered. By providing a model of persuasion as it occurs most profoundly, in honest vernacular, through urgent and personal dialectic, the preacher "woos the audience," as Burke would say, through a kind of indirect courtship. Preachers who are also pastors are supposed to love their congregations, and this love is expressed in a willingness to seduce, by example, those who share the compulsion to be fitfully married to the Gospel.

There is a way of talking that is intimate and inclusive and that becomes, by virtue of its high regard for the listener, a rhetorical version of the self-fulfilling prophecy. It sounds like this: "You've all seen it . . . you know exactly how it feels . . . there's not a one of you sitting here this morning that has not at one time or another felt exactly what I am feeling." This is called the "rhetoric of regard," of respect, of ingratiation. Call it what you will, it pronounces us good before we yet are. And in this way, like the Gospel, it helps to make us that way. Chaim Perleman wrote once, "The speaker will make every effort to conciliate his audience, either by showing his solidarity with it or his esteem for it by demonstrating his trust in its judgment."[20]

The preacher who practices the art of a pygmalion rhetoric knows that sometimes you have to jump start a listener. If you don't get him talking to himself, then self-persuasion will not occur, and if you don't know how to talk to yourself on his behalf, then he has no model to imitate, no dialectic into which he can move vicariously. Sometimes it is in being told that one is listening carefully, as carefully as the preacher is listening to himself, that one is swept along almost unwittingly into the preacher's conversation. In certain moments, when the roles are nearly indistinguishable, what Burke calls "cosubstantiality" has occurred. That fleeting thing called pure persuasion may be approached only when the listener isn't sure who is talking anymore.

The art of pygmalion rhetoric is not so much a certain style or collection of phrases as it is a mind-set. It seeks to close the experiential and rhetorical world of the speaker and listener by constantly insisting that the gap is very small, even nonexistent. The self-persuading preacher delights in making her listener feel like a partner in the persuasion process, not the object of it. She may have a good head start in conversing with the text, but she wants company to finish the job—good company, wise and thoughtful company.

Gradually, over time, the self-persuading preacher and the congregation become partners in the experience that is the sermon. The congregation knows from the outset that the sermon is a trip and not just a destination. Furthermore, they will travel along, vicariously, to places the preacher has visited but wants to return to, this time with friends. Human beings by nature feel affection and respect for those who *consider* them, who factor their feelings and fears into their formulas for meaningful communication. The self-persuading preacher never forgets to expect more of the listener than is reasonable, so that he will get more from them than even they thought possible. This is how a self-persuading preacher ends up with a self-persuading congregation.

Envy and the Holy Spirit

A minister remembers one Fourth of July when, as a child, he made that sacred journey to buy fireworks. The tents near his home sprang up like mirages; they existed for only a week or two, displaying their fantastic wares to wide-eyed children. They catered to the pyromaniac in all of us. The shelves were loaded with brightly wrapped potential fire, smoke, noise, and danger, all disguised as little gifts with tissue-paper covers and Chinese script. Were it not for the intoxicating smell of gunpowder, and the world's briefest but most exciting instructions—LIGHT FUSE, GET AWAY—the tent could have been selling paper cranes and cricket boxes.

The most difficult part was making decisions about what to buy. Ten dollars went fast, even in those days, and it was important to stretch that allowance over the widest possible range of what gun powder and cardboard could do. You can't tell a good firework by its cover, so the boy took three different samples to the counter for a further explanation of their capacities.

The teenager running the cash register looked enormous and wise, and the boy was certain that he was an expert in fireworks, perhaps even a connoisseur of pyrotechnics. Maybe he worked here for free just to be around the goods. Maybe he was the world's leading expert on the stationary three-color fountain; or the only man ever to have had a roman candle go off in his face and live to tell about it. Maybe he knew the secret formula that made Black Cats the BMW of firecrackers. Who knows? *He* knows!

The three items were placed on the counter, and the boy, who was nine, looked up into the face of the looming guru who sold these wonderful, dangerous things to minors. "What does this one do?" he asked.

"It goes up," came the reply in a flat, uninterested voice.

"And what about *this* one?" the lad continued, hoping for a little more energy in the answer.

"It pops."

After a moment of silence, during which those standing in line shifted impatiently and made throat-clearing noises that meant "Move it kid!" the boy pushed one last, best hope in front of the cashier. It was the largest of them all. It had a heavy, waxed green fuse that marked it as being in the illicit power class of the old (and now illegal) M-80s. "What does *this* one do?" he asked almost plaintively.

"It goes up *and* pops . . . look kid, are you going to buy anything?"

That little boy who would someday become a preacher gathered up the items that had once looked like treasure and now looked small and overpriced and returned them to the shelf. When he walked out of the shade of the tent into the bright sunlight he realized somehow that buying fireworks would never be the same.

That memory, on the surface nothing more than a bit of nostalgia, illustrates the tragedy of the loss of passion in preaching. Because we all possess a primal memory, a sense that we are from God and to God, human beings still wander into churches and feel the strange quickening of the spirit that comes in the temple light. We sense that we are in the presence of something incomprehensible, beyond us and yet paradoxically for us. There is a quiet in us that wants to shout, and a shouting in us that wants to be quiet. When it comes time for the sermon, we look up and see someone who must know the secrets of this place; its power and potential. And we hold our breath, because before he speaks our expectations are so high. Please, we say to ourselves almost plaintively, say something besides that you are for God and against sin, Amen.

In a classic piece of writing, novelist Fred Beuchner describes this same expectant moment when people wonder if in the midst of all the words, they will hear the Word:

> In the front pews the old ladies turn up their hearing aids, and a young lady slips her six-year-old a Life Saver and a Magic Marker. A college sophomore home for vacation who is there because he was dragged there, slumps forward with his chin in his hand. The vice-president of a bank who twice this week has seriously considered suicide places his hymnal in the rack. A pregnant girl feels the life stir inside her. A high school teacher, who for twenty years has managed to keep his homosexuality a secret for the most part even from himself, creases his order of service down the center with his thumbnail and tucks it under his knee. . . . The preacher pulls the little cord that turns on the lectern light and deals out his note cards like a river boat gambler. The stakes have never been higher. Two minutes from now he may have lost his listeners completely to their own thoughts, but at this moment he has them in the palm of his hand. The silence in the shabby church is deafening because everybody is listening to it. . . . Everybody knows the kinds of things he has told them before and not told them, but who knows what this time, out of the silence, he will tell them.[21]

Imagine what it might mean to preaching if ministers felt this much excitement, this much anticipation, about hearing their own sermons? When they stood to read Scripture, for example, the voice would betray the excitement one feels when opening an envelope containing the names of the winners of some contest or award. And even though they are on intimate terms with the passage, they would never read it as if all its meaning has been spent. The conversation has been private until this moment, but there is something about going public. Telling it again means hearing it again. Hearing it again means experiencing the passion that made it worth the telling. If this is the posture of the self-persuading preacher, then the sermon will not disappoint those who, in the deafening silence of that shabby church, wait for a word from God.

Strange as it may sound, preaching as self-persuasion is designed to cause a healthy sort of *envy* in the listener. Not the kind that corrupts, or eats up the spirit alive, but the kind that genuinely wants what only passion can give to life. Week after week, the pews are filled with people who come wondering what sort of perpetual energy source keep the preacher going. Why, when this is such a relentless obligation, with so many Sundays stretching into infinity, does the self-persuading preacher seem to grow stronger and believe more deeply?

The answer, of course, is that she is the first beneficiary of all her work. She is delighted to know where good preaching can be found and good listeners can be made. The impact on all those other listeners is no less profound. They feel as we all do when sitting next to someone in a restaurant who is relishing a dish and can't keep quiet about it. When the waitress comes by, we are likely to say: "I'll have what she's having."

Lip Sync and the Communion of the Saints

A fascinating thing occurred once at a meeting of the Academy of Homiletics. This professional group is made up of teachers of preaching, and they gather once a year to talk homiletic theory, discuss papers, and even take their turn in the pulpit before a demanding audience. One of the academy's recent guests was a full-blooded Choctaw Indian from Oklahoma. He was addressing the group about American Indian stereotypes that persist in both society and the church. As he spoke, something odd but interesting was happening to one of his listeners—

something that illustrates perfectly the vicarious nature of human communication and speaks volumes about self-persuasion.

The listener was a homiletics professor and a preacher of national reputation. He was standing in the back of the room, because all the seats were taken. As the guest talked with passion and imagination about his predicament, the professor could be seen moving his lips a mile a minute. He had the appearance of a man in a trance, talking to himself without making any audible sounds. Whatever it was he was doing, he was completely and unself-consciously absorbed in it. Several of his colleagues observed him and commented on it later: "What was he doing?" He was self-persuading.

The impulse in human beings to put an experience into their own words is so powerful, especially among gifted communicators, that it can occur almost simultaneously with the experience itself. When human speech moves us profoundly, when emotions are stirred, and the imagination quickens us to insight, we want to talk about it, attach our own phrases to it, and even practice the sound of it on ourselves. Likewise, we almost always think of someone that we wish to relate the experience to, and we begin at once to rehearse the narrative, to choose the words, to prepare our telling in such a way that it will do justice to the experience:

> Have you ever noticed how much of "what" we experience is shaped by the anticipation of "how" we will share it with someone? You did not listen across the Austrian Alps for the fivefold echo of your own "hello," you did not coax your daughter into her first step, you did not lean against the rail and stare into the fog for the first glimpse of the Statue of Liberty, and then sometime later think of communicating the experience. Were you not at the very time of the experiences already searching for the words, phrases, analogies to go into the journal, the letter, the phone call?[22]

Talking to oneself is not a sign of eccentricity but rather a normal outgrowth of the intricate relationship between the emotions and the vocal cords, the hypnotic spell of ideas upon the gatekeeper of one's own voice and the habits of the heart compelling its restless companion the tongue. Those who delight in language are especially susceptible to the habit of mumbling their

way through a world that wants to be, begs to be, verbally constituted. Sound, as Alfred N. Whitehead reminded us, is the natural symbol for the deep experiences of existence, and speech is
human nature itself without the artificiality of writing. No wonder he said, "Expression is the one fundamental human sacrament."[23]

Watching the professor at the meeting move his lips and delight in the ideas that moved his tongue and animated his face
unaware was like watching a cameo of the whole concept of self-
persuasion. He could have been doing many different things:
translating and paraphrasing the speaker's words to give them
relevance and immediacy; anticipating a speech or sermon he
would give into which this conversation would now surely in-
trude; or simply engaging the speaker's ideas as dialectic, arguing
another point of view, conversing with the mind of his guest for
the sake of clarity, and checking himself for the sound of his own
opinion. Whatever he was doing, he was enjoying it. Between
the words he was hearing the speaker say, and the words he was
hearing himself say, he had quite a conversation going.

Think for a moment, once more, how important this phenomenon is for the self-persuading preacher. The call to preach requires that one repeatedly converse with Scripture that, though
poignant, concrete, and full of pathos, often does not speak
clearly and forcefully to the modern ear. To study these texts for
the purpose of preaching requires the art of an almost simul-
taneous translation. That is, the self-persuading preacher will
have to move his lips a lot.

Meanwhile, out in the congregation during the sermon it is
often the case that lips are moving also, unaware. Sensing that
the sermon is bigger than anyone in the room, and that it is
consuming the preacher on their behalf, the listeners lean forward and let the words move their faces. Some of them even
begin moving their mouths—not necessarily to repeat what they
are hearing but to start putting it into their own words. How else
are they going to explain this sermon to their friend who slept in,
or to their colleague who gave up on church long ago, or even to
themselves, since they are often unsure about a lot of things?

Perhaps they are protesting, getting ready to shake the preacher's hand and to politely disagree. Or perhaps they have let the sermon slip past the guard they keep up to protect them from uncommon opinion, and they are startled at their own conversation. Or perhaps they are role-playing a new vision, describing how it feels to be someplace where they have never been before. Could they be trying to talk themselves into returning home, or are they remembering that you can't go home again? Whatever it is, those moving lips are a precious sight to the preacher.

Who knows, if all this lip-syncing got out of hand, and grew from a whisper to a murmur, and from a murmur to a song, someone might write about it some day. They might describe it as the "rush of a mighty wind," as if the whole church was caught up in contagious self-persuasion.

They might even call it Pentecost.

Notes

Introduction

1. Herbert W. Simmons, "Persuasion and Attitude Change," in *Speech Communication Behavior: Perspectives and Principles*, ed. Larry L. Barker and Robert J. Kibler (Englewood Cliffs, N.J.: Prentice Hall, 1971), 232.

Chapter One

1. Saint Augustine, *On Christian Doctrine*, trans. D. W. Robertson (Indianapolis: Bobbs-Merrill, 1958).

2. Fred B. Craddock, *Overhearing the Gospel* (Nashville: Abingdon Press, 1978), 10.

3. *The Rhetoric of Aristotle: A Translation* (Cambridge University Press, 1909), 5.

4. Don Wardlaw, *Preaching Biblically: Creating Sermons in the Shape of Scripture* (Philadelphia: Westminster Press, 1983), 6.

5. Douglas Ehninger, "On Systems of Rhetoric," *Philosophy and Rhetoric* 1 (Summer 1968): 131–44.

6. George Campbell, *The Philosophy of Rhetoric* (Boston: Charles Ewer, 1823), 101.

7. Mary John Smith, *Persuasion and Human Action* (Belmont, Calif.: Wadsworth Publishing Co., 1983), 7.

8. See Richard E. Petty, Thomas M. Ostrom, and Timothy C. Brock, eds., *Cognitive Responses in Persuasion* (Hillsdale, N.J.: Lawrence Erlbaum, 1984); Richard M. Perloff and Timothy C. Brock, "'And Thinking Makes It So': Cognitive Responses in Persuasion," in *Persuasion: New Directions in Theory and Research*, ed. Michael E. Roloff and Gerald R. Miller (Beverly Hills: Calif.: Sage Publications, 1980), 67–99; and Anthony G. Greenwald, "Cognitive Learning, Cognitive Response to Persuasion, and Attitude Change," in *Psychological Foundations of Attitudes*, ed. Anthony G. Greenwald, Timothy C. Brock, and Thomas M. Ostrom (New York: Academic Press, 1968), 147–70.

9. For a summary of Tesser's research, see Abraham Tesser, "Self-Generated Attitude Change," *Advances in Experimental Social Psychology* 9 (1973): 236–45.

Chapter Two

1. Thomas Oden, ed., *The Parables of Kierkegaard* (Princeton: Princeton University Press, 1978), 71.
2. R. E. C. Browne, *The Ministry of the Word* (Philadelphia: Fortress Press, 1958), 73.
3. Walter Ong, *Orality and Literacy* (New York: Methuen, 1983), 12.
4. Martin Heidegger, *Existence and Being*, trans. Stefan Schimanski (Chicago: Henry Regnery, 1949), 270 (emphasis mine).
5. Craddock, *Overhearing the Gospel*, 25.
6. Georges Gusdorf, *Speaking*, trans. Paul T. Brockelman (Evanston: Northwestern University Press, 1965), 119–27.
7. For a thorough discussion of this concept, see Fred B. Craddock, *Preaching* (Nashville: Abingdon Press, 1985), 52–65.
8. See Robert N. Gaines, "Doing by Saying: Toward a Theory of Perlocution," *Quarterly Journal of Speech* 65 (1979): 207–17.
9. Alfred N. Whitehead, *Modes of Thought* (New York: Capricorn Books, 1938), 45–57.
10. See Daryl Bem, "Self-Perception Theory," *Advances in Experimental Social Psychology* 1 (1965): 199–218.

Chapter Three

1. The Yale approach to persuasion is detailed in Carl I. Hovland, Irving L. Janis, and Harold H. Kelley, *Communication and Persuasion* (New Haven: Yale University Press, 1953).
2. For a full explanation of what remains one of the most important single refutations of conventional sermonic structure based on Aristotelian outlining, read Fred B. Craddock's *As One without Authority: Essays on Inductive Preaching* (Enid, Okla.: Phillips University Press, 1974), especially chapter three.
3. Craddock, *Preaching*, 25–26.
4. Ibid., 97.
5. Kenneth Burke, *A Rhetoric of Motives* (New York: Prentice Hall, 1950), 55.

Chapter Four

1. The complete treatment of the concept of "overhearing" can be found in Craddock, *Overhearing the Gospel.*

2. William D. Thompson, ed., *Preaching Biblically: Exegesis and Interpretation* (Nashville: Abingdon Press, 1981), 14.

3. James D. Smart, *The Past, Present, and Future of Biblical Theology* (Philadelphia: Westminster Press, 1979), 43.

4. David Buttrick, *Homiletic: Moves and Structures,* (Philadelphia: Fortress Press, 1987), 265.

5. To get at the thought of Rudolph Bultmann, readers may wish to begin with *Jesus Christ and Mythology* (New York: Scribners, 1958) and then turn to *Existence and Faith* (New York: Meridian, 1960).

6. Suzanne Langer, "On Cassier's Theory of Language and Myth," in *The Philosophy of Ernst Cassier,* ed. Paul Schlipp (New York: Tudor Publishing, 1949), 387–90.

7. Craddock, *Overhearing the Gospel,* 69.

8. J. Lynch, *The Broken Heart: The Medical Consequences of Loneliness* (New York: Basic Books, 1977), 239–42.

9. Browne, *The Ministry of the Word,* 98.

Chapter Five

1. William Watts, "Relative Persistence of Opinion Change Induced by Active compared to Passive Participation," *Journal of Personality and Social Psychology* 5 (1967): 4–15.

2. Edward M. Bodaken, Timothy G. Plax, Richard W. Piland, and Allen N. Weiner, "Role Enactment as a Socially Relevant Explanation of Self-Persuasion," *Human Communication Research* 5 (1979): 203–14.

3. Bem, "Self-Perception Theory."

4. William Barrett, *Irrational Man: A Study in Existential Philosophy* (New York: Heinemann, 1961), 72.

5. Søren Kierkegaard, *Concluding Unscientific Postscript,* trans. David Swenson and Walter Lowrie (Princeton: Princeton University Press, 1941), 339.

6. Leslie Weatherhead, *The Christian Agnostic* (Nashville: Abingdon, 1965), 55.

7. Stanley Fish, *Self-Consuming Artifacts* (Berkley: University of California Press, 1971), x.

8. Craddock, *Overhearing the Gospel*, 131.

9. See Henry Mitchell, *The Recovery of Preaching* (San Francisco: Harper & Row, 1977).

10. Ibid., 162.

11. Paul Holmer, "Kierkegaard and Theology," *Union Seminary Quarterly Review* 12 (1957): 26.

12. Mircea Eliade, *Patterns in Comparative Religion*, trans. Rosemary Sheed (New York: Sheed & Ward, 1958), 434.

13. Mitchell, *The Recovery of Preaching*, 32.

14. Ibid., 18–19.

Chapter Six

1. Thomas Benson and Michael Prosser, eds., *Readings in Classical Rhetoric* (Bloomington: Indiana University Press, 1969), 57.

2. Ibid., 118.

3. Craddock, *Preaching*, 24.

4. Ronald D. Laing, *The Divided Self* (New York: Penguin Books, 1965).

5. Erik Erikson, *Identity, Youth, and Crisis* (New York: W. W. Norton, 1968).

6. Browne, *The Ministry of the Word*, 41.

7. William Sloane Coffin, Jr., comment made during Minister's Week at Phillips University, Enid, Okla., January 1979.

8. Burke, *A Rhetoric of Motives*, 22.

9. Ibid., 269.

10. Hans Van Der Geest, *Presence in the Pulpit: The Impact of Personality in Preaching*, trans. Douglas W. Scott (Atlanta: John Knox Press, 1981), 83.

11. Browne, *The Ministry of the Word*.

12. Ibid., 97.

Chapter Seven

1. Buttrick, *Homiletic*, 173.

2. Browne, *The Ministry of the Word*, 55.

3. Craddock, *Preaching*, 89.

4. Excerpt from a student speech delivered at the University of Oklahoma, Fall 1989.

5. John Macquarrie, *Martin Heidegger* (Richmond: John Knox Press, 1968), 48.

6. Craddock, *As One without Authority*, 78.

7. Browne, *The Ministry of the Word*, 59.

8. Ibid., 69.

9. Austin Farr, *A Rebirth of Images* (Dacre Press, 1949), 19–20.

10. Heidegger, *Existence and Being*, 270.

11. R. E. C. Browne, *The Ministry of the Word*, 27.

12. Ignor Stravinsky, *Poetics of Music in the Form of Six Lessons* (Cambridge: Harvard University Press, 1970), 87.

13. Craddock, *As One without Authority*, 94–95.

14. Browne, *The Ministry of the Word*, 24.

15. Ibid., 40.

16. Craddock, *Preaching*, 203.

17. Kenneth Burke, "Counter-Statement," in James Golden, Goodwin Berquist, and William Coleman, eds., *The Rhetoric of Western Thought*, 4th ed. (Dubuque: Kendall Hunt, 1989), 320.

18. Kenneth Burke, "The Philosophy of Literary Form," in Golden, Berquist, and Coleman, *The Rhetoric of Western Thought*, 320.

19. Kenneth Burke, "Rhetoric—Old and New," *The Journal of General Education* 5 (April 1951): 203.

20. Brian Wicker, *The Story-Shaped World* (Notre Dame: University of Notre Dame Press, 1975), 47.

21. Craddock, *Overhearing the Gospel*, 135.

22. Ibid., 137.

23. Browne, *The Ministry of the Word*, 93.

24. Ibid.

25. Buttrick, *Homiletic*, 194.

Chapter Eight

1. Golden, Berquist, and Coleman, *The Rhetoric of Western Thought*, 98.

2. Ibid., 99.

3. *Commentarius Cantabrigiensis in Epistolas Pauli e Schola Petri Abaelardi: In Epistolam ad Romanos*, ed. A. Landgraf (Notre Dame: University of Notre Dame Press, 1937), 1–2.

4. See Michael Meyer, "Dialetic and Questioning: Socrates and Plato," *American Philosophical Quarterly* 17 (October 1980): 283.

5. Sir Frederick Bartlett is generally credited with originating the notion of cognitive schemata. See Frederick C. Bartlett, *Remembering: A Study in Experimental and Social Psychology* (London: Cambridge University Press, 1932).

6. I. A. Richards, "Emotive Language Still," *The Yale Review* 38 (Autumn 1949): 108–18.

7. Ibid.

8. For an excellent summation of contemporary trends in persuasion theory and research, see Smith, *Persuasion and Human Action*, 309–18.

9. T. B. Rogers, N. A. Kuiper, and W. S. Kirker, "Self-Reference and the Encoding of Personal Information," *Journal of Personality and Social Psychology* 35 (1977): 677.

10. See N. A. Kuiper, T. B. Rogers, Lee Ross, Donald Snygg, and Arthur W. Combs, *Individual Behavior: A Perceptual Approach to Behavior* (New York: Harper & Row, 1959).

11. See "Plato's Theory of Dialectic" in Golden, Berquist, and Coleman, *Rhetoric of Western Thought*, 28.

12. See Stephen W. Littlejohn, *Theories of Human Communication*, 2d ed. (Belmont, Calif.: Wadsworth Publishing Co., 1983), 147–49.

13. Craddock, *Overhearing the Gospel*, 130.

14. Littlejohn, *Theories of Human Communication*, 57.

15. See Leon Festinger, "A Theory of Social Comparison Processes," *Human Relations* 7 (1954): 117–40; and George R. Goethals and John M. Darley, "Social Comparison Theory: An Attitudinal Approach," in *Social Comparison Processes: Theoretical and Empirical Perspectives*, ed. Jerry M. Suls and Richard L. Miller (Washington, D.C.: Hemisphere Publishing Co., 1977), 259–78.

16. Albert Bandura, *Social Learning Theory* (Morristown, N.J.: General Learning Press, 1971), 2.

17. Leon Festinger, *A Theory of Cognitive Dissonance* (Evanston, Ill.: Row, Peterson, 1957), 13.

18. Jacob L. Moreno, *Who Shall Survive?* 2d ed. (New York: Beacon House, 1953).

19. George A. Kelly, *The Psychology of Personal Constructs* (New York: W. W. Norton, 1955).

20. Leon Mann, "The Effects of Emotional Role-Playing on Desire to Modify Smoking Habits," *Journal of Experimental Social Psychology* 3 (1967): 334–48.

21. Richard Weaver, *The Ethics of Rhetoric* (Chicago: Henry Regnery, 1970), 17.

Chapter Nine

1. Charles L. Bartow, *The Preaching Moment: A Guide to Sermon Delivery* (Nashville: Abingdon Press, 1980), 15.

2. Ibid., 14.

3. M. L. Huffman, "Empathy, Its Development and Prosocial Implications," in *Nebraska Symposium on Motivation*, vol. 25, *Social Cognition Development*, ed. H. E. Howe and C. B. Keasey (Lincoln: University of Nebraska Press, 1977), 169–217.

4. Golden, Berquist, and Coleman, *The Rhetoric of Western Thought*, 397.

5. Kenneth Burke, *Permanence and Change* (New York, 1935), 71.

6. Browne, *The Ministry of the Word*, 23.

7. Walter J. Ong, *The Presence of the Word* (New Haven: Yale University Press, 1967), 117–22.

8. Burke, *Permanence and Change*, 71.

9. S. M. Berger, "Conditioning through Vicarious Instigation," *Psychological Review* 69, 450–66.

10. W. A. Beardslee, *Literary Criticism of the New Testament* (Philadelphia: Fortress Press, 1970), 9.

11. Paul Ricoeur, "Biblical Hermeneutics," *Semeia* 4 (1975): 67.

12. E. D. Hirsch, *Validity in Interpretation* (New Haven: Yale University Press, 1967), ix-x.

13. Browne, *The Ministry of the Word*, 47.

14. John Bluck, *Beyond Neutrality: A Christian Critique of the Media* (Geneva, Switzerland: World Council of Churches, 1978), 25.

15. Craddock, *As One without Authority*, 85.

16. Reuel Howe, *Partners in Preaching: Clergy and Laity in Dialogue* (New York: Seabury Press, 1967), 35.

17. Albert Bandura, "Social Learning Perspective on Behavior Change," in *What Makes Behavior Change Possible?* ed. A. Burton (New York: Brunnel/Mazel, 1976), 34–57.

18. Richard Weaver uses this theme as the basic thrust of his opening essay, "The Phaedrus and the Nature of Rhetoric," in *The Ethics of Rhetoric* (Chicago: Henry Regnery Co., 1953).

19. Aristotle, *Rhetoric*, 2.4.

20. Chaim Perelman and L. Olbrechts-Tyteca, *The New Rhetoric: A Treatise on Argumentation* (Notre Dame: Notre Dame University Press, 1969), 320.

21. Frederick Buechner, *Telling the Truth* (New York: Harper & Row, 1977), 22–23.

22. Craddock, *Overhearing the Gospel*, 17.

23. Alfred N. Whitehead, *Religion in the Making* (New York: Macmillan, 1926), 131.

Selected Bibliography

Communication Theory

Alexander, Hubert. *Language and Thinking*. Princeton, N.J.: Van Nostrand, 1967.

Allport, G. W. *Personality: A Psychological Interpretation*. New York: Holt, 1937.

Alston, W. P. *Philosophy of Language* Englewood Cliffs, N.J.: Prentice-Hall, 1964.

Benthall, J., and T. Polhemus, eds. *The Body as a Medium of Expression*. New York: Dutton, 1975.

Berger, Peter, and Thomas Luckmann. *The Social Construction of Reality*. Garden City, N.Y.: Doubleday, 1966.

Berlo, David K. *The Process of Communication*. New York: Holt, Rinehart, & Winston, 1960.

Binkley, Timothy. *Wittgenstein's Language*. The Hague: Martinus Nijhoff, 1973.

Black, Max. *Models and Metaphors*. Ithaca, N.Y.: Cornell University Press, 1962.

Blummer, Herbert. "Attitudes and the Social Act." *Social Problems* 3 (1955):59–65.

Bois, J. Samuel. *The Art of Awareness*. Dubuque, Ia.: W. C. Brown, 1966.

Bormann, Ernest G. *Communication Theory*. New York: Holt, Rinehart, & Winston, 1980.

Boulding, Kenneth. *The Image*. Ann Arbor: University of Michigan Press, 1956.

Brummett, Barry. "Some Implications of 'Process' or 'Intersubjectivity': Postmodern Rhetoric." *Philosophy and Rhetoric* 9 (1976): 21–51.

Bruner, J. S., Jacquelin J. Goodnow, and G. A. Austin. *A Study of Thinking*. New York: John Wiley & Sons, 1956.

Burke, Kenneth. *Attitudes toward History*. New York: New Republic, 1937.

_____. *Counter-Statement.* New York: Harcourt, Brace, 1931.

_____. *A Grammar of Motives.* Englewood Cliffs, N.J.: Prentice-Hall, 1945.

_____. *Language as Symbolic Action.* Berkeley and Los Angeles: University of California Press, 1966.

_____. *Permanence and Change.* New York: New Republic, 1935.

_____. *The Philosophy of Literary Form.* Baton Rouge: Louisiana State University Press, 1941.

_____. *A Rhetoric of Motives.* New York: Prentice Hall, 1950.

_____. *A Rhetoric of Religion.* Boston: Beacon Press, 1961.

Campbell, Paul N. "A Rhetorical View of Locutionary, Illocutionary, and Perlocutionary Acts." *Quarterly Journal of Speech* 59 (1973): 284–96.

Cassier, Ernst. *An Essay on Man.* New Haven: Yale University Press, 1944.

_____. *The Philosophy of Symbolic Forms.* 3 vols. Berlin: Bruno Cassirer, 1923, 1925, 1929.

Chomsky, Noam. *Language and Mind.* New York: Harcourt Brace Jovanovich, 1972.

_____. *Reflections on Language.* New York: Pantheon Books, 1975.

Couch, Carl J. and Robert Hintz, eds. *Constructing Social Life.* Champaign, Ill.: Stipes Publishing Co., 1975.

Cronen, Vernon Pearce, W. Barnett, and Linda Harris. "The Logic of the Coordinated Management of Meaning." *Communication Education* 28 (1979): 22–38.

Dance, Frank E. X., and Carl E. Larson. *The Function of Human Communication: A Theoretical Approach.* New York: Holt, Rinehart, & Winston, 1976.

Dance, Frank., ed. *Human Communication Theory: Comparative Essays.* New York: Harper & Row, 1982.

Deetz, Stanley. "Words without Things: Toward a Social Phenomenology of Language." *Quarterly Journal of Speech* 59 (1973): 40–51.

Delia, Jesse. "Alternative Perspectives for the Study of Human Communication: Critique and Response." *Communication Quarterly* 25 (1977): 54.

_____. *Symbols and Society.* New York: Oxford University Press, 1968.

Dittmann, Allen T. *Interpersonal Messages of Emotion.* New York: Springer, 1972.

DeVito, Joseph A., ed. *Language: Concepts and Processes.* Englewood Cliffs, N.J.: Prentice-Hall, 1973.

Dewey, John. *Art as Experience.* New York: Minton, Blach, 1934.

———. *Experience and Nature*. Chicago: Open Court, 1925.

Ekman, Paul, and Wallace Friesen. *Emotion in the Human Face: Guidelines for Research and an Integration of Findings*. New York: Springer, 1972.

Fisher, Aubrey B. *Perspectives on Human Communication*. New York: Macmillan, 1978.

Gaines, Robert. "Doing by Saying: Toward a Theory of Perlocution." *Quarterly Journal of Speech* 65. (1979): 207–17.

Goffman, Erving. *Behavior in Public Places*. New York: Free Press, 1963.

———. *Interaction Ritual: Essays on Face-to-Face Behavior*. Garden City, N.Y.: Doubleday, 1967.

———. *Relations in Public*. New York: Basic Books, 1971.

Hall, Edward T. *The Hidden Dimension*. New York: Random House, 1966.

Harrison, Bernard. *An Introduction to the Philosophy of Language*. New York: St. Martin's Press, 1979.

Harvey, John K., William J. Ickes, and Robert F. Kidd, eds., *New Directions in Attribution Research*. 2 vols. New York: John Wiley & Sons, 1976, 1978.

Hayakawa, S. I. *Language in Thought and Action*. New York: Harcourt, Brace, 1952.

———. *On the Way to Language*. New York: Harper & Row, 1971.

Hovland, Carl I., Irving Janis, and Harold Kelley. *Communication and Persuasion*. New Haven: Yale University Press, 1953.

Hovland, Carl I., et al. *The Order of Presentation in Persuasion*. New Haven: Yale University Press, 1959.

Janis, Irving, et al. *Personality and Persuasibility*. New Haven: Yale University Press, 1959.

Johannesen, Richard L., ed. *Contemporary Theories of Rhetoric*. New York: Harper & Row, 1971.

Jones, Edward E., et al. *Attribution: Perceiving the Causes of Behavior*. Morristown, N.J.: General Learning Press, 1972.

Jourard, Sidney. *Disclosing Man to Himself*. New York: Van Nostrand Reinhold, 1968.

———. *Self-Disclosure: An Experimental Analysis of the Transparent Self*. New York: John Wiley & Sons, 1971.

———. *The Transparent Self*. New York: Van Nostrand, 1971.

Katz, Jerrold J. *The Philosophy of Language*. New York: Harper & Row, 1966.

Katz, Jerrold. *The Underlying Reality of Language and Its Philosophical Import*. New York: Harper & Row, 1971.

Kinch, John W. "A Formalized Theory of the Self-Concept." *The American Journal of Sociology* 68 (1963): 481–86.

Kuhn, Manford H., and Thomas S. McPartland. "An Empirical Investigation of Self-Attitudes." *American Sociological Review* 19 (1954): 68–76.

Kuhn, Thomas S. *The Structure of Scientific Revolutions.* Chicago: University of Chicago Press, 1970.

Laing, R. D. *The Politics of Experience.* New York: Pantheon, 1967.

————. *Self and Others.* London: Tavistock, 1969.

Langer, Susanne. *Mind: An Essay on Human Feeling.* 3 vols. Baltimore: Johns Hopkins Press, 1967.

————. "On Cassier's Theory of Language and Myth." In *The Philosophy of Ernst Cassirer,* edited by Paul Schlipp, 387–90. New York: Tudor Publishing, 1949.

————. *Philosophy in a New Key.* Cambridge: Harvard University Press, 1942.

Lee, Irving J. *Language Habits in Human Affairs.* New York: Harper & Brothers, 1941.

Littlejohn, Stephen W. *Theories of Human Communication.* 2d ed. Belmont, Calif.: Wadsworth Publishing Co., 1983.

Manis, Melvin. *Cognitive Processes.* Monterey, Calif.: Brooks/Cole, 1966.

Mead, George H. *Mind, Self, and Society.* Chicago: University of Chicago Press, 1934.

————. *The Philosophy of the Act.* Chicago: University of Chicago Press, 1938.

Miller, George, ed. *Communication, Language, and Meaning.* New York: Basic Books, 1973.

Needham, Rodney. *Belief, Language, and Experience.* Chicago: University of Chicago Press, 1973.

Newcomb, Theodore. *The Acquaintance Process.* New York: Holt, Rinehart, & Winston, 1961.

Ogden, C. K., and I. A. Richards. *The Meaning of Meaning.* London: Kegan, Paul Trench, Trubner, 1923.

Osgood, Charles. *Cross Cultural Universals of Affective Meaning.* Edited by James Snider and Charles Osgood. Urbana: University of Illinois Press, 1975.

————. "On Understanding and Creating Sentences." *American Psychologist* 18 (1963): 735–51.

Osgood, Charles, George Suci, and Percy H. Tannenabaum. *The Measurement of Meaning.* Urbana: University of Illinois Press, 1957.

Pearce, W. Barnett, and Vernon Cronen. *Communication Action and Meaning.* New York: Praeger, 1980.

Piaget, Jean. *The Construction of Reality in the Child.* New York: Basic Books, 1954.

Pfeutze, Paul E. *The Social Self.* New York: Bookman Associates, 1954.

Reardon, Kathleen. *Persuasion: Theory and Context.* Beverly Hills, Calif.: Sage Publications, 1981.

Reeves, Joan W. *Thinking about Thinking.* London: Martin Secher and Warburg, 1965.

Reitman, Walter R. *Cognition and Thought.* New York: John Wiley & Sons, 1965.

Richards, I. A. *The Philosophy of Rhetoric.* New York: Oxford University Press, 1936.

Rokeach, Milton. *Beliefs, Attitudes, and Values: A Theory of Organization and Change.* San Francisco: Jossey-Bass, 1969.

Rokeach, Milton. "Persuasion that Persists." *Psychology Today,* September 1971, 68.

Schutz, Alfred. *The Phenomenology of the Social World.* Translated by George Walsh and Frederick Lehnert. Evanston, Ill.: Northwestern University Press, 1967.

Schutz, William. *Elements of Encounter.* New York: Bantam, 1975.

Searle, John. "Human Communication Theory and the Philosophy Language: Some Remarks." In *Human Communication Theory,* edited by Frank Dance, 116–29. New York: Holt, Rinehart, & Winston, 1967.

Sherif, Muzafer. *The Psychology of Ego-Involvements.* New York: John Wiley & Sons, 1947.

———. *Social Interaction: Process and Products.* Chicago: Aldine, 1967.

Simons, Herbert. "The Carrot and Stick as Handmaidens of Persuasion in Conflict Situations." In *Perspectives on Communication in Social Conflict,* edited by Gerald Miller and Herbert Simons, 172–205. Englewood Cliffs, N.J.: Prentice-Hall, 1974.

Smith, Dennis R., and Lawrence Kearney. "Organismic Concepts in the Unification of Rhetoric and Communication." *Quarterly Journal of Speech* 59 (1973): 30–39.

Solso, R. L., ed. *Theories of Cognitive Psychology.* Hillsdale, N.J.: Erlbaum, 1974.

Staats, Arthur. *Learning, Language, and Cognition.* New York: Holt, Rinehart, & Winston, 1968.

Steiner, Claude. *Scripts People Live.* New York: Grove Press, 1974.

Weimer, W. B., and D. S. Palermo, eds. *Cognitions and the Symbolic Process*. Hillsdale, N.J.: Erlbaum, 1974.

Whorf, Benjamin L. *Language, Thought, and Reality*. New York: John Wiley & Sons, 1956.

Wilmot, William. "Meta-communication: A Reexamination and Extension." In *Communication Yearbook*, vol. 4, edited by Dan Nimmo. New Brunswick, N.J.: Transaction Books, 1980.

Persuasion Theory

Allport, Gordon W. "Attitudes." In *Handbook of Social Psychology*, edited
by C. Murchison. Worcester, Mass.: Clark University Press, 1935.

Ajzen, Icek. "Attitudinal vs. Normative Messages: An Investigation of the Differential Effects of Persuasive Communications on Behavior." *Sociometry* 34 (1971): 263–280.

Anderson, Kenneth E. *Persuasion: Theory and Practice*. Boston: Allyn & Bacon, 1971.

Aristotle. *The Rhetoric of Aristotle*. Cambridge: Cambridge University Press, 1909.

Barnlund, Dean C. "A Transactional Model of Communication." In *Language Behavior: A Book of Readings*, edited by Johnnye Akin et al., 53–71. The Hague: Mouton, 1970.

Baron, Reuben M. "Attitude Change through Discrepant Action: A Functional Analysis." In *Psychological Foundations of Attitudes*, edited by Anthony G. Greenwald, Timothy C. Brock, and Thomas M. Ostrom, 297–326. New York: Academic Press, 1968.

Bandura, Albert. *Social Foundations of Thought and Action*. Englewood Cliffs, N.J.: Prentice-Hall, 1986.

———. *Social Learning Theory*. Morristown, N.J.: General Learning Press, 1971.

Baron, Robert A. "Attraction toward the Model and Model's Competence as Determinants of Adults' Imitative Behavior." *Journal of Personality and Social Psychology* 14 (1970): 345–51.

Bauer, Raymond A. "The Obstinate Audience: The Influence Process from the Point of View of Social Communication." *American Psychology* 19 (1964): 319–28.

Bem, Daryl J. *Beliefs, Attitudes, and Human Affairs*. Monterey, Calif.: Brooks/Cole, 1970.

———. "Self-Perception Theory." In *Advances in Experimental Social Psychology* 1 (1965): 199–218.

Benwar, Carl, and Edward L. Deci. "Attitude Change as a Function of the Inducement for Espousing a Proattitudinal Communication." *Journal of Experimental Social Psychology* 11 (1975): 271–78.

Berger, Charles R., and Richard J. Calabrese. "Some Explorations in Initial Interaction and Beyond: Toward a Developmental Theory of Interpersonal Communication." *Human Communication Research* 1 (1975): 99–112.

Berscheid, Ellen. "Opinion Change and Communicator-Communicatee Similarity and Dissimilarity." *Journal of Personality and Social Psychology* 4 (1966): 670–80.

Bettinghaus, Erwin P. *Persuasive Communication.* 3d ed. New York: Holt, Rinehart, & Winston, 1980.

Bodaken, Edward M., Timothy G. Plax, Richard W. Piland, and Allen N. Weiner, "Role Enactment as a Socially Relevant Explanation of Self-Persuasion." *Human Communication Research* 5 (1979): 203–14.

Brehm, Jack W. *A Theory of Psychological Reactance.* New York: Academic Press, 1966.

Brembeck, Winston L., and William S. Howell. *Persuasion: A Means of Social Change.* 2d ed. Englewood Cliffs, N.J.: Prentice-Hall, 1976.

Brockriede, Wayne. "Toward a Contemporary Aristotelian Theory of Rhetoric." *Quarterly Journal of Speech* 54, (1968): 1–12.

Burgoon, Michael, Marshall Cohen, Michael D. Miller, and Charles L. Montgomery, "An Empirical Test of a Model of Resistance to Persuasion." *Human Communication Research* 4 (1978): 27–29.

Burnstein, Eugene, and Amiran Vinokur. "Persuasive Argumentation and Social Comparison as Determinants of Attitude Polarization." *Journal of Experimental Social Psychology* 13 (1977): 315–32.

Cohen, Arthur. *Attitude Change and Social Influence.* New York: Basic Books, 1964.

———. "An Experiment on Small Rewards for Discrepant Compliance and Attitude Change." In *Explorations in Cognitive Dissonance,* edited by Jack W. Brehm and Arthur R. Cohen, 73–78. New York: John Wiley, 1962.

Cronkite, Gary. *Persuasion-Speech and Behavioral Change.* Indianapolis, Ind.: Bobbs-Merrill, 1969.

Doob, Leonard W. "The Behavior of Attitudes." *Psychological Review* 54 (1947): 135–56.

Duval, Shelley, and Robert A. Wichlund. *A Theory of Objective Self-Awareness.* New York: Academic Press, 1972.

Eagly, Alice H., and Samuel Himmelfarb. "Current Trends in Attitude Theory and Research." In *Readings in Attitude Change,* edited by Samuel Himmelfarb and Alice Hendrickson Eagly, 594–610. New York: John Wiley, 1947.

Elashoff, Janet D., and Richard E. Snow. *Pygmalion Reconsidered.* Worthington, Ohio: Charles A. Jones, 1971.

Fehrenback, Peter A., David J. Miller, and Mark H. Thelen. "The Importance of Consistency of Modeling Behavior upon Imitation: A Comparison of Single and Multiple Models." *Journal of Personality and Social Psychology* 37 (1979): 1412–17.

Festinger, Leon. *A Theory of Cognitive Dissonance.* Evanston, Ill.: Row, Peterson, 1957.

Festinger, Leon, and Elliot Aronson. "The Arousal and Reduction of Dissonance in Social Contexts." In *Group Dynamics,* edited by Dorwin Cartwright and Alvin Zander, 214–31. New York: Harper & Row, 1960.

Fishbein, Martin, and Icek Ajzen. *Belief, Attitude, Intention, and Behavior.* Reading, Mass.: Addison-Wesley, 1975.

Fotheringham, Wallace C. *Perspectives on Persuasion.* Boston: Allyn & Bacon, 1966.

Golden, James L., Goodwin F. Berquist, and William E. Coleman. *The Rhetoric of Western Thought.* 4th ed. Dubuque, Ia.: Kendall Hunt, 1989.

Greenwald, Anthony G. "Cognitive Learning, Cognitive Response to Persuasion, and Attitude Change." In *Psychological Foundations of Attitudes,* edited by Anthony G. Greenwald, Timothy C. Brock, and Thomas M. Ostrom, 147–70. New York: Academic Press, 1968.

Gross, Alan E., Barbara S. Riemer, and Barry E. Collins. "Audience Reaction as a Determinant of the Speaker's Self-Persuasion." *Journal of Experimental Social Psychology* 9 (1973): 246–56.

Himmelfarb, Samuel, and Allikce Hendrickson Eagly, eds. *Readings in Attitude Change.* New York: John Wiley, 1974.

Hovland, Carl I., and Wallace Mandell. "Is There a 'Law of Primacy in Persuasion'?" In *The Order of Presentation in Persuasion,* edited by Carl I. Hovland et al., 13–22. New Haven: Yale University Press, 1957.

Hovland, Carl I., and Walter; Weiss. "The Influence of Source Credibility on Communication Effectiveness." *Public Opinion Quarterly* 15 (1951): 635–50.

Hovland, Carl I., Arthur A. Lumsdaine, and Fred D. Sheffield. "The Effects of Presenting 'One Side' versus 'Both Sides' in Changing Opinions on a Controversial Subject." In *Experiments on Mass Communication*, 201–27. Princeton, N.J.: Princeton University Press, 1949.

Janis, Irving L., and J. Barnard Gilmore. "The Influence of Incentive Conditions on the Success of Role Playing in Modifying Attitudes." *Journal of Personality and Social Psychology* 1 (1965): 17–27.

Janis, Irving L., and Leon Mann. "Effectiveness of Emotional Role-Playing in Modifying Smoking Habits and Attitudes." *Journal of Experimental Research in Personality* 1 (1965): 84–90.

Janis, Irving, et al. *Personality and Persuasibility*. New Haven: Yale University Press, 1959.

Johannesen, Richard L., ed. *Ethics and Persuasion: Selected Readings*. New York: Random House, 1967.

Johannesen, Richard. *Contemporary Theories of Rhetoric*. New York: Harper & Row, 1971.

Jones, Edward E., and Keith E. Davis. "From Acts to Dispositions: The Attribution Process in Person Perception." In *Advances in Experimental Social Psychology*, edited by E. Leonard Berkowitz. New York: Academic Press, 1965.

Katz, Daniel, Irving Sarnoff, and Charles McCllintock. "Ego-Defense and Attitude Change." *Human Relations* 9 (1956): 27–45.

Kelman, Herbert C. "Attitudes Are Alive and Well and Gainfully Employed in the Sphere of Action." *American Psychologist* 29 (1974): 310–24.

Knowler, Franklin R. "Experimental Studies of Changes in Attitudes: A Study of the Effect of Oral Argument on Changes of Attitude." *Journal of Abnormal and Social Psychology* 6 (1935): 315–47.

Langer, Ellen J. "Rethinking the Role of Thought in Social Interaction." In *New Direction in Attribution Research*, edited by John H. Harvey, William Ickes, and Robert F. Kidd, 35–58. Hillsdale, N.J.: Lawrence Erlbaum, 1978.

Larson, Charles U. *Persuasion: Reception and Responsibility*. 2d ed. Belmont, Calif.: Wadsworth Publishing Co., 1979.

Lerbinger, Otto. *Designs for Persuasive Communication*. Englewood Cliffs, N.J.: Prentice-Hall, 1972.

Linder, Darwyn E., Joel Cooper, and Edward E. Jones. "Decision Freedom as a Determinant of the Role of Incentive Magnitude in Attitude Change." *Journal of Personality and Social Psychology* 6 (1967): 39–45.

Lund, Frederick Hansen. "The Psychology of Belief: A Study of its Emotional and Volitional Determinants." *Journal of Abnormal and Social Psychology* 20 (1925): 174–96.

McGuire, William J. "The Concept of Attitudes and Their Relations to Behaviors." In *Perspective on Attitude Assessment: Surveys and Their Alternatives*, edited by E. H. Wallace Sinaiko and L. A. Broedlin. Champaign, Ill.: Pendleton, 1976.

———. "Personality and Susceptibililty to Social Influence." In *Handbook of Personality Theory and Research*, edited by E. F. Borgatta and W. W. Lambert. Chicago: Rand McNally, 1967.

———. "The Relative Efficacy of Various Types of Prior Belief-Defense in Producing Immunity against Persuasion" *Journal of Abnormal and Social Psychology* 63 (1961): 327–37.

Miller, Gerald R. "On Being Persuaded: Some Basic Definitions." In *Persuasion: New Directions in Theory and Research*, edited by Michael E. Roloff and Gerald R. Miller, 11–38. Beverly Hills, Calif.: Sage Publications, 1980.

Miller, Gerald R., and Michael Burgoon. *New Technique of Persuasion.* New York: Harper & Row, 1973.

———. "Persuasion Research: and Commentary." In *Communication Yearbook 2*, edited by Brent D. Ruben, 29–47. New Brunswick, N.J.: Transaction Books, 1978.

Mills, Judson, and Eliot Aronson. "Opinion Change as a Function of the Communicator's Attractiveness and Desire to Influence." *Journal of Personality and Social Psychology* 1 (1965): 173–77.

Minnick, Wayne C. *The Art of Persuasion.* Boston: Houghton Mifflin, 1968.

Nel, Elizabeth, Robert Helmreich, and Eliot Aronson. "Opinion Change in the Advocate as a Function of the Persuasibility of His Audience: A Clarification of the Meaning of Dissonance." *Journal of Personality and Social Psychology* 12 (1969): 117–24.

Newcomb, Theodore. "An Approach to the Study of Communicative Acts." *Psychological Review* 60 (1953): 393–404.

Nuttin, Jozef M., Jr. *The Illusion of Attitude Change: Toward a Response Contagion Theory of Persuasion.* London: Academic Press, 1975.

Pearce, W. Barnett, and Vernon E. Cronen. *Communication, Action, and Meaning: The Creation of Social Realities.* New York: Praeger, 1980.

Perloff, Richard M., and Timothy C. Brock. "'And Thinking Makes It So': Cognitive Responses in Persuasion." In *Persuasion: New Directions In Theory and Research*, edited by Michael E. Roloff and

Gerald R. Miller, 67–99. Beverly Hills, Calif.: Sage Publications, 1980.

Petty, Richard E. and John T. Cacioppo. "Issue Involvement Can Increase or Decrease Persuasion by Enhancing Message-Relevant Cognitive Responses." *Journal of Personality and Social Psychology* 37 (1979): 1915–26.

Reardon, Kathleen Kelley. *Persuasion: Theory and Context.* Beverly Hills, Calif.: Sage Publications, 1981.

Regan, Dennis T., and Russell Fazio. "On the Consistency between Attitudes and Behavior: Look to the Method of Attitude Formation." *Journal of Experimental Social Psychology* 13 (1977): 28–45.

Rokeach, Milton. *Beliefs, Attitudes, and Values.* San Francisco: Jossey-Bass, 1968.

Roloff, Michael E. "Self-Awareness and the Persuasion Process: Do We Really Know What We're Doing?" In *Persuasion: New Directions in Theory and Research,* edited by Michael E. Roloff and Gerald R. Miller, 29–66. Beverly Hills Calif.: Sage Publications, 1980.

Rosenbaum, Milton E., and Irving F. Tucker. "Competence of the Model and the Learning of Imitation and Nonimitation." *Journal of Experimental Psychology* 63 (1962): 183–90.

Rosenthal, Robert, and Lenore Jacobson. *Pygmalion in the Classroom: Teacher Expectations and Pupils' Intellectual Development.* New York: Holt, Rinehart, & Winston, 1968.

Scheidel, Thomas M. *Persuasive Speaking.* Glenview, Ill.: Schoot, Foresman, 1967.

Schlenker, Barry R., and Marc Riess. "Self-Persuasion of Attitudes Following Commitment to Proattitudinal Behavior." *Human Communication Research* 5 (1979): 325–34.

Schramm, Wilbur. "The Nature of Communication Between Humans." In *The Process and Effects of Mass Communication,* edited by Wilbur Schramm and Donald F. Roberts, 3–53. Urbana, Ill.: University of Illinois Press, 1981.

Scott, William A. "Attitude Change by Response Reinforcement: Replication and Extension." *Sociometry* 22 (1959): 328–35.

Sherif, Muzafer, and Hadley Cantril. *The Psychology of Ego-Involvements.* New York: John Wiley, 1947.

Smith, Mary John. *Persuasion and Human Action.* Belmont, Calif.: Wadsworth Publishing Co., 1983.

Stang, David J. "The Effects of Mere Exposure on Learning and Affect." *Journal of Personality and Social Psychology* 31 (1975): 7–13.

Tarde, Gabriel. *The Laws of Imitation* New York: Holt, 1903.

Tesser, Abraham. "Self-Generated Attitude Change." *Advances in Experimental Social Psychology* 31 (1975): 262–70.

Tesser, Abraham, and Christopher Leone. "Cognitive Schemata and Thought as Determinants of Attitude Change." *Journal of Experimental Social Psychology* 13 (1977): 340–56.

Watts, William A. "Relative Persistence of Opinion Change Induced by Active Compared to Passive Participation." *Journal of Personality and Social Psychology* 5 (1967): 4–15.

Weiss, Robert Frank. "Persuasion and the Acquisition of Attitudes: Models from Conditioning and Selective Learning." *Psychological Reports* 11 (1962): 709–32.

Wheeler, Ladd. "Toward a Theory of Behavioral Contagion." *Psychological Review* 73 (1966): 179–92.

Whorf, Benjamin L. "The Relations of Habitual Thought and Behavior to Language." In *Language, Thought, and Reality*, edited by John B. Carroll, 135–59. Cambridge, Mass.: MIT Press, 1956.

Wilmot, William W. *Dyadic Communication: A Transactional Perspective*. Reading, Mass.: Addison-Wesley, 1975.

Zimbardo, Philip G., Matisyohu Weisenberg, Ira Firestone, and Burton Levy. "Communicator Effectiveness in Producing Public Conformity and Private Attitude Change." *Journal of Personality and Social Psychology* 33 (1965): 233–55.

Homiletic Theory

Abbey, Merrill R. *Communication in Pulpit and Parish*. Philadelphia: Westminster Press, 1973.

———. *Preaching to the Contemporary Mind*. Nashville: Abingdon Press, 1963.

———. *The Word Interprets Us*. New York: Abingdon Press, 1962.

Achtemeier, Elizabeth. *Creative Preaching: Finding the Words*. Nashville: Abingdon Press, 1980.

———. *Preaching as Theology and Art*. Nashville: Abingdon Press, 1984.

Allen, Ronald J. *Our Eyes Can Be Opened: Preaching the Miracle Stories of the Synoptic Gospels Today*. Washington D.C.: University Press of America, 1982.

Atkins, G. Glenn. *Preaching and the Mind of Today*. New York: Round Table Press, 1934.

Augustine, Saint. *On Christian Doctrine*. Translated by D. W. Robertson. Indianapolis: Bobbs-Merrill, 1958.

Barth, Karl. *Homiletik: Weren Und Vorbereitung der Predigt*. Zurich: Evz-Verlag, 1966.

_____. *The Preaching of the Gospel*. Translated by B. E. Hooke. Philadelphia: Westminster Press, 1963.

Bartlett, Gene. *The Audacity of Preaching*. New York: Harper, 1962.

Bartow, Charles L. *The Preaching Moment: A Guide to Sermon Delivery*. Nashville: Abingdon Press, 1980.

Baxter, Batsell Barrett. *The Heart of the Yale Lectures*. New York: MacMillan, 1947.

Best, Ernest. *From Text to Sermon: Responsible Use of the New Testament in Preaching*. Atlanta: John Knox Press, 1978.

Blackwood, Andrew Watterson. *The Preparation of Sermons*. New York: Abingdon/Cokesbury, 1948.

Bohren, Rudolf. *Preaching and Community*. Translated by David Green. Richmond: John Knox Press, 1965.

Broadus, John Albert. *On the Preparation and Delivery of Sermons*. Revised edition. New York and London: Harper Brothers, 1944.

Brown, David M. *Dramatic Narrative in Preaching*. Valley Forge, Pa.: Judson Press, 1981.

Browne, R. E. C. *The Ministry of the Word*. Philadelphia: Fortress Press, 1958.

Buechner, Frederick. *Telling the Truth: the Gospel as Tragedy, Comedy, and Fairy Tale*. New York: Harper & Row, 1977.

Buttrick, David. *Homiletic: Moves and Structures*. Philadelphia: Fortress Press, 1987.

Chartier, Myron R. *Preaching as Communication: An Interpersonal Perspective*. Nashville: Abingdon Press, 1981.

Cox, James William. *A Guide to Biblical Preaching*. Nashville: Abingdon Press, 1976.

_____. *Preaching: A Comprehensive Approach to the Design and Delivery of Sermons*. San Francisco: Harper & Row, 1985.

Craddock, Fred B. *As One without Authority: Essays on Inductive Preaching*. Enid, Okla.: Phillips University Press, 1974.

_____. *Overhearing the Gospel*. Nashville: Abingdon Press, 1978.

_____. *Preaching*. Nashville: Abingdon Press, 1985.

Davis, Henry Grady. *Design For Preaching*. Philadelphia: Muhlenberg Press, 1958.

Edwards, O. C. *The Living and Active Word: One Way to Preach from the Bible Today*. New York: Seabury Press, 1975.

Eggold, Henry J. *Preaching Is Dialogue: A Concise Introduction to Homiletics*. Grand Rapids, Mich.: Baker Book House, 1980.

Eslinger, Richard L. *A New Hearing: Living Options in Homiletic Methods*. Nashville: Abingdon Press, 1987.

Fant, Clyde E. *Preaching for Today*. New York: Harper & Row, 1975.

Fischer, Wallace E. *Who Dares to Preach?: The Challenge of Biblical Preaching*. Abingdon Press, 1968.

Fitzgerald, George R. *A Practical Guide to Preaching*. New York: Paulist Press, 1980.

Freeman, Harold. *Variety in Biblical Preaching: Innovation Techniques and Fresh Forms*. Waco, Tex.: Word Books, 1987.

Fuller, Reginald H. *The Use of the Bible in Preaching*. Philadelphia: Fortress Press, 1981.

Garrison, Webb B. *Creative Imagination in Preaching*. New York: Paulist Press, 1980.

Geest, Hans Van Der. *Presence in the Pulpit: The Impact of Personality on Preaching*. Translated by Douglas W. Scott, Atlanta: John Knox Press, 1981.

Greidomus, Sidney. *The Modern Preacher and the Ancient Text: Interpreting and Preaching Biblical Literature*. Grand Rapids, Mich.: Eerdmans, 1988.

Hall, Thor. *The Future Shape of Preaching*. Philadelphia: Fortress Press, 1971.

Halvorson, Arndt L. *Authentic Preaching*. Minneapolis, Minn.: Augsburg Publishing House, 1982.

Howard, J. Grant, *Creativity in Preaching*. Grand Rapids, Mich.: Ministry Resources Library, 1987.

Howe, Reuel. *Partners in Preaching: Clergy and Laity in Dialogue*. New York: Seabury Press, 1967.

Jabusch, Willard. *The Person in the Pulpit: Preaching as Caring*. Nashville: Abingdon Press, 1980.

Jensen, Richard A. *Telling the Story: Variety and Imagination in Preaching*. Minneapolis, Minn.: Augsburg Publishing House, 1980.

Keck, Leander E. *The Bible in the Pulpit: The Renewal of Biblical Preaching*. Nashville: Abingdon Press, 1978.

Kemper, Deane A. *Effective Preaching: A Manuel for Students and Pastors*. Philadelphia: Westminster Press, 1985.

Killinger, John. *The Centrality of Preaching in the Total Ministry of the Church*. Waco, Tex.: Word Books, 1969.

———. *Fundamentals of Preaching*. Philadelphia: Fortress Press, 1985.

Killinger, John, ed. *Experimental Preaching*. Nashville: Abingdon Press, 1973.

Knoche, H. Gerald. *The Creative Task: Writing the Sermon*. St. Louis: Concordia Publishing House, 1977.

Lischer, Richard. *A Theology of Preaching: The Dynamics of the Gospel*. Nashville: Abingdon Press, 1981.

Liske, Thomas. *Effective Preaching*. 2d ed. New York: Macmillan, 1960.

Long, Thomas G. *The Senses of Preaching*. Atlanta: John Knox Press, 1988.

Lowry, Eugene L. *Doing Time in the Pulpit: The Relationship between Narrative and Preaching*. Nashville: Abingdon Press, 1985.

————. *The Homiletical Plot: The Sermon as Narrative Art Form*. Atlanta: John Knox Press, 1980.

Lueking, F. Dean. *Preaching: The Art of Connecting God and People*. Waco, Tex.: Word Books, 1985.

McCraken, Robert J. *The Making of the Sermon*. New York: Harper & Brothers, 1956.

MacLeod, Donald. *Here is My Method: The Art of Sermon Construction*. Westwood, N.J.: F. H. Revell, 1952.

Malcomson, William L. *The Preaching Event*. Philadelphia: Westminister Press, 1968.

Marty, Martin E. *The Word: People Participating in Preaching*. Philadelphia: Fortress, 1984.

Massey, James E. *Designing the Sermon: Order and Movement in Preaching*. Nashville: Abingdon Press, 1980.

Muehl, William. *Why Preach? Why Listen?* Philadelphia: Fortress Press, 1986.

Nichols, J. Randall. *Building the Word: The Dynamics of Communication and Preaching*. San Francisco: Harper & Row, 1980.

Oden, Thomas C. *Ministry through Word and Sacrament*. New York: Crossroads, 1988.

Pike, James A. *A New Look in Preaching*. New York: Scribners, 1961.

Proctor, Samuel. *Preaching about Crisis in the Community*. Westminster Press, 1988.

Rahner, Hugo. *A Theology of Proclamation*. Translated by Richard Dimmler. New York: Herder & Herder, 1968.

Randolph, David James. *The Renewal of Preaching*. Philadelphia: Fortress Press, 1969.

Read, David H. *Preaching about the Real Needs of People*. Philadelphia: Westminister Press, 1988.

Reid, Clyde H. *The Empty Pulpit: A Study in Preaching as Communication*. New York: Harper & Row, 1967.

Reierson, Gary B. *The Art of Preaching: The Intersection of Theology, Worship, and Preaching with the Arts.* Lanham, Md.: University Press of America, 1988.

Rice, Charles. *Interpretation and Imagination: The Preacher and Contemporary Literature.* Philadelphia: Fortress Press, 1970.

Rust, Eric C. *The Word and Words: Toward a Theology of Preaching.* Macon, Ga.: University Press, 1982.

Salmon, Bruce C. *Storytelling in Preaching.* Nashville: Broadman Press, 1988.

Sanders, James A. *God Has a Story Too: Sermons in Context.* Philadelphia: Fortress Press, 1979.

Scherer, Paul. *For We Have This Treasure.* New York: Harper & Brothers, 1944.

Sider, Ronald J. *Preaching about Life in a Threatening World.* Philadelphia: Westminster Press, 1987.

Skudlarek, William. *The Word in Worship: Preaching in a Liturgical Context.* Nashville: Abingdon Press, 1981.

Sleeth, Ronald. *God's Word and Our Words: Basic Homiletics.* Atlanta: John Knox Press, 1986.

Steimle, Edmund A. *Preaching the Story.* Philadelphia: Fortress Press, 1980.

Swank, George. *Dialogical Style in Preaching.* Nashville: Abingdon Press, 1966.

Thompson, William D. *A Listener's Guide to Preaching.* Nashville: Abingdon Press, 1966.

————. *Preaching Biblically: Exegesis and Interpretation.* Nashville: Abingdon Press, 1981.

Troeger, Thomas. *Creating Fresh Images for Preaching: New Rungs for Jacob's Ladder.* Valley Forge: Judson Press, 1982.

Van Seters, Arthur, ed. *Preaching as a Social Act: Theology and Practice.* Nashville: Abingdon Press, 1988.

Wardlaw, Don. *Preaching Biblically: Creating Sermons in the Shape of Scripture.* Philadelphia: Westminster Press, 1983.

Welsch, Clement. *Preaching in a New Key: Studies in the Psychology of Thinking and Listening.* Philadelphia: United Church Press, 1974.

Willimon, William. *Integrative Preaching: The Pulpit at the Center.* Nashville: Abingdon Press, 1981.

Index